MEMORIES OF THE PRESENT

A SOCIOLOGICAL CHRONICLE OF IRELAND
1997–1998

Also in this series:

*Encounters with Modern Ireland: A Sociological
    Chronicle 1995–1996*
    edited by Michel Peillon and Eamonn Slater,
    Dublin: Institute of Public Administration, 1998.

Irish Sociological Chronicles
volume 2 (1997–98)

MEMORIES OF THE PRESENT

A SOCIOLOGICAL CHRONICLE OF IRELAND
1997–1998

Edited by Eamonn Slater and Michel Peillon

Images from Susan Gogan and Derek Knight

IPA
INSTITUTE OF PUBLIC
ADMINISTRATION

First published 2000
by the Institute of Public Administration
57-61 Lansdowne Road
Dublin 4

ISBN 1 902448 29 4
ISSN 1393-7464

British Library Cataloguing in Publication Data
A catalogue record for this book is available from the
British Library

Cover design by Creative Inputs, Dublin
Origination by Wendy Commins, The Curragh
Printed in Ireland by Future Print, Dublin

Contents

Contributors

Alan BAIRNER, University of Ulster
Brendan BARTLEY, National University of Ireland, Maynooth
Colm BREATHNACH, National University of Ireland,
  Maynooth
David CAIRNS, National University of Ireland, Maynooth
Ruth CASEY, National University of Ireland, Maynooth
Farrel CORCORAN, Dublin City University
Mary P. CORCORAN, National University of Ireland,
  Maynooth
Colin COULTER, National University of Ireland, Maynooth
Eoin DEVEREUX, University of Limerick
Ciara KIERANS, National University of Ireland, Maynooth
Maria LOHAN, Trinity College, Dublin
Agnès MAILLOT, Dublin City University
Philip McCORMACK, National University of Ireland,
  Maynooth
Paddy O'CARROLL, University College Cork
Richard O'LEARY, The Queen's University of Belfast
Seán Ó RIAIN, University of California
Sara O'SULLIVAN, University College Dublin
Michel PEILLON, National University of Ireland, Maynooth
A. Jamie SARIS, National University of Ireland, Maynooth
Eamonn SLATER, National University of Ireland, Maynooth
Jim SMYTH, The Queen's University of Belfast
Alex WHITE, Barrister-at-Law
James WICKHAM, Trinity College, Dublin

Images and photographs:

Preface

This book, the second in the series *Irish Sociological Chronicles*, covers the years 1997 and 1998. In Ireland, these two years have been marked by continued economic progress in the south and by significant steps towards the resolution of the violent conflict in the north. Crucially, the perception that Ireland has of itself and the image that it projects outside have been greatly transformed during these two years. This book highlights some aspects of this transformation.

We would like to think that each of the analyses that are presented in this book contributes to the construction of the intellectual tools through which features of Irish society can be understood. In a sense, Ireland has outgrown the frames of reference according to which it was interpreted. The series, in a modest way, participates in the task of reshaping our analytical tools. This is done around particular events or topics which form the focus of each chapter. As editors, we aimed at providing a medium through which ideas about Ireland can be tried and explored, with little concern for orthodoxy, and put across as clearly as possible to a wide readership.

A particular effort has been made on the visual presentation of the book. Not only are the images printed in colour but, more significantly, we obtained the co-operation of professional photographers. Daniel de Chenu, head of the photography department at the Dún Laoghaire Institute of Art, Design and Technology, has from the start backed this project and participated in it. Susan Gogan and Derek Knight have together produced most of the images in the book, and we are grateful for their contribution. All this would not have been possible without the help of Professor Liam Ryan, of the Department of Sociology at NUI Maynooth. We also wish to acknowledge the support of the Jean Monnet Project, European Commission.

The Institute of Public Administration has been most supportive of our endeavour. Tony McNamara has listened patiently to our sometimes odd suggestions and responded positively to most of them. Our thanks must finally go to our contributors who have, in their various ways, reflected on aspects of Ireland in 1997 and 1998. The ideas they express remain, of course, their own and the editors do not necessarily share them. But they all offer analyses which enhance our understanding of contemporary Ireland. They have become *memories of an Irish present*.

Introduction

This book covers topics and issues that came to the fore in Ireland during 1997 and 1998. These were memorable years, that is to say worthy of being remembered. They marked the assertion of a new Ireland. The slow and difficult unfolding of a peace process in Northern Ireland occupies a central place in this context. Paradoxically, this process became memorable because it demanded that the past be forgotten: the four hundred years of history, the thirty years of extreme enmity and violence, the atrocities, the wounds and the deaths. How indeed could the protagonists in the Northern Irish conflict continue to remember without confronting each other? Memorable too for the continuing economic boom in Ireland and, more significantly, the realisation that new found prosperity, however fragile, can no longer be construed as a mere blip, a momentary quirk of history. During these two years Ireland came to terms with its new economic prosperity and started to celebrate it. But it also experienced difficulties generated by the new prosperity, of which housing and traffic appear prominent, along with the deepening of social divisions and the marginalisation of the poor and unskilled. Finally, the depth of corruption in some sectors of the economic and political elite was made ever more glaring by each media revelation and each tribunal of inquiry. The antics of the past are once more returning to haunt the existence of the living.

A fair amount of remembering has been done in Ireland in the last few years, with the commemoration of a range of significant past events. Remembering the past – and deciding

3

on what to remember as well as how to remember it – constitutes a way of sustaining the present, of fixing contemporary points of reference, of defining oneself. The present is about remembering in another way: many events in these two years have set themselves up as significant markers and even, one may well muse, as objects of future commemoration. These present features constituted themselves, from the start, as memories, as something whose main function is to be remembered. In its staging, the peace process in Northern Ireland followed such a logic: every new step was hailed as a 'first ever' and this historical character was used to ensure progress in the negotiations. Such a process was expected to culminate in a momentous and symbolic end to 'the Troubles'. That it did not happen at the time does not alter the emphasis of the whole process on constructing itself as something to remember.

A chronicle records what is worth retaining in the collective memory, only to relegate into oblivion what is, quite simply, not recorded. Keeping a record becomes in this way a form of forgetting. It is of course a lot easier to forget than to remember, for the latter requires an active recognition. One usually forgets by default rather than by choice. This contingent character of remembering and forgetting reveals itself in this book. Some important aspects of life in Ireland during these two years, 1997 and 1998, are not included in our collection: ours is not a systematic memory. But, more essentially, the grid of relevance is changing all the time. Occurrences or trends that are not registered today, which do not even reach the threshold of awareness, may soon acquire a formidable significance. One would like to claim for this book that it is pointing to processes and happenings in Ireland which are only beginning to trigger this awareness, that it focuses on aspects of the present which need to be remembered because they already pertain to an Irish future. All this, however, should not lead us to deny that groups and societies engage in an active forgetting: that they sometimes refuse to acknowledge events that they find difficult to deal with.

4

Memory and identity

As a sociological chronicle of Ireland during 1997 and 1998, this book does not simply provide a record of significant events. It attempts to reach deeper; to place such occurrences into a broader context; it seeks to give reasons for them. Remembering, in sociological terms, implies that we identify and analyse the processes which unfold in and shape the present.

The first part of the book deals with the issue of memory through which past and present are tightly connected. The commemoration of the 1798 uprising is observed by Paddy O'Carroll in 'Re-membering 1798'. The state remained the main player in these commemorations, but other groups participated in them in an effort to promote their preferred memory of the events. The chapter presents the stories these various participants wanted to tell about 1798 and how they chose to remember it.

Farrel Corcoran, in 'Technologies of memory', focuses on some of the mechanisms through which memories are produced and identities constructed. He looks more particularly at the issue of immigration to Ireland and examines the role of the mass media in this production of memory. But memory also suggests its reverse: amnesia. The author recalls how Ireland simply forgot some unedifying aspects of its past and he highlights some of the mechanisms through which unwelcome memories can be revived and confronted.

When memories bolster an ideology that sustains a clear social hierarchy, they turn into a way of not seeing the present. Colin Coulter, in 'The orange order of things', outlines the core ideas of the unionist viewpoint, with its strong emphasis on universal values and rationality. He ponders on the apparent inability of unionists to acknowledge the momentous transformations that have taken place in southern Ireland. This does not mean that the unionist ideology is not changing. It is in fact moving away from upholding a universalist emphasis to becoming the defence of a particular identity.

The 'curse of memory' is not such that it makes impossible a renegotiation of the past. Sinn Féin, as the main political expression of republicanism, has engaged in a process of metamorphosis. In 'Reinventing Sinn Féin', Agnès Maillot argues that Sinn Féin, or at least its leadership, endeavours to position itself in the political systems of both north and south. The republican identity is being redefined at a time when its commitment to pursue the armed struggle is decreasing. In so doing, it faces the difficult task of forging a new balance between nationalist goals and social radicalism.

The slow transformation of inter-group relations in Northern Ireland reveals itself, in part, in relation to sport. The support for particular sports or for particular teams has long functioned in Northern Ireland as a marker of identity; as a statement about the group to which one belongs and about the allegiance one professes. Alan Bairner, in 'Sport and peace: an uneasy dialogue', wonders if the boundaries that are traced around the different ethnic identities continue to fuel the conflict or if they are slowly dissolving to bring people together across the sectarian divide.

The trouble with prosperity

During the two years which this chronicle covers, southern Ireland has settled into the new perception of itself as a successful and dynamic society. The metaphor of the Celtic Tiger has become somewhat overdrawn, but economic indices have nonetheless continued to record growth beyond expectations. This growing prosperity intensified deep divisions between those who were in a position to ride the economic tide and those who were left far behind. It also generated new problems.

James Wickham and Maria Lohan, in 'Dublin's car system', use a comparative study of Athens, Bologna, Dublin and Helsinki to assess the reasons for the acute traffic problems experienced in Dublin. They lay the blame on the weak governance of Dublin, where fragmented local authorities enjoy no autonomy in taking responsibility for the urban environment.

The multiplication of suburban shopping centres follows

6

the same logic of urban development. But the development of these suburban shopping malls has required the active participation of local and central public authorities. Mary Corcoran, in 'Mall city', identifies the main features of this new means of consumption. She particularly emphasises the ambiguity of malls that, as private spaces, endeavour to present themselves as quasi-public spaces.

The growing number of immigrants in Ireland directly results from its economic development. This immigration has triggered a hostile reaction in some quarters. Against an analysis which stresses the rejection of cultural differences, Michel Peillon argues, in 'Strangers in our midst', that this hostility is largely determined by the conditions in which immigrants are made to live in Irish society.

Other groups of people are left out of this economic prosperity. 'Horses and the culture of protest in west Dublin', by A. Jamie Saris et al., highlights the resistance which is offered by youths to the determination of local public authorities to regulate tightly the ownership and care of horses in Cherry Orchard. Through their opposition to the introduction of rules and regulations that are hostile to their world, they uphold a culture which they value and which defines them. In the process, their resistance reveals the kind of power which is exercised against them.

The significant economic development that has taken place, mainly in the second half of the 1990s, was at first met with incredulity. But this new reality has slowly dawned and become a cause for celebration. The visits of the Tour de France and the Tall Ships have provided Irish people with occasions for engaging in celebratory festivities. In 'Carnival Ireland', Michel Peillon looks at some of the ways Ireland celebrates the new era. Festive celebrations occupy a significant place in this context and they become a kind of unproductive expenditure through which a troublesome economic surplus is dissipated. The celebratory urge expresses itself further in the making of heroes, through whom Ireland exalts its accomplishment. Mary Robinson has been constructed into such a heroic figure.

Contested reflexivity

In *Encounters with Modern Ireland*, the first volume in this series, several contributions pointed to the growth of reflexivity. This refers to the ability of groups, institutions and society as a whole to reflect on and monitor their activity in a self-conscious way. It was suggested that societies overcome some of the problems they confront through increased reflexivity. But caution was also urged about viewing such a development as general or one-sided. Not all aspects of social life experience this increasing reflexivity, and in any case the latter should not be seen as straightforward. The exploration of the theme of reflexivity is continued in the third part of this book. The emphasis is set on reflexivity as a contested development, as a site of struggle.

Richard O'Leary, in 'The President's Communion', interprets President Mary McAleese taking the Anglican Communion at Christ Church as a highly symbolic act, which challenged the unquestioning attitude that is required of Catholics in the practice of their faith. He shows that an increasing number of followers deviate from church rules on this issue and on others. Catholic believers are adopting an increasingly questioning attitude towards their church, and they meet with resistance from within the church itself.

The popularity of radio phone-ins and talk shows is investigated by Sara O'Sullivan in 'Talk radio'. Talk radio represents, at least in part, a mechanism through which norms, particularly of sexual practices, are considered collectively, reflected upon and in some way confirmed or rejected. Radio talk shows provide a space where new identities are explored, negotiated and elaborated in a fairly self-conscious way. But in the battle over audience ratings, these shows soon adopt predictable formulae. Their commodified nature seriously restricts the reflexive potential of such programmes.

Ireland generates an enormous mass of information about itself, and this is duly reported in the media. This does not imply that Irish society produces this information to monitor itself. Michel Peillon, in 'Information overgrowth', develops the view that this growth is best interpreted as a mechanism which closes off reflexivity.

Similarly, Mary Corcoran and Alex White, in 'Irish democracy and the tribunals of inquiry', look critically at the increasing reliance on tribunals of inquiry in Irish public life. Such tribunals are established mainly as a response to a major crisis in the political system and to overcome a serious erosion of legitimacy. Furthermore, the media have transformed such tribunals into sensationalist spectacles. They conclude that such tribunals of inquiry do not promote the kind of democratic debate which would be the mark of a reflexive society.

Embedded global processes

Global processes operate beyond the locality, the region, and the nation-state. This is not a new phenomenon, although it has become extensive and thorough as more and more aspects of social life are moulded by these large processes. But they are not unfolding within an empty space and their effect occurs at the interface of local situations, where they encounter the resistance which is offered by already established structures and processes. In a sense, the locality provides the substance of global processes, the material on which they work. As they embed themselves in local situations in order to have an impact on them, they also receive at their very core the imprint of the locality. Global processes are best understood in their confrontation with local structures and processes, which clearly reveal their nature and their dynamic. For this reason, the idea that global processes are shaping Ireland today is not a very interesting statement, if it leads to a neglect of local structures and processes. The contributions contained in the last part of this collection present a series of studies dealing with the close interaction between global and local.

Eoin Devereux, in 'A media famine', shows how a global issue has been reported in Ireland. The reporting of famines in the Third World depends to a large extent on information generated and diffused by global news agencies and broad-casting organisations. But the local media appropriate these global issues, through a localised logic of news production. This chapter sets out to demonstrate how local factors and dynamics play an important role in the way global processes are experienced and impact on the locality.

Embracing global entities at the local level is considered by Eamonn Slater in 'The archaeology of Irish golfscapes', where he discusses how some Irish golfscapes adopted the now global design of the American course. This style is being determined by a new perspective, one which is itself determined by a new technology of seeing: the television panoramic view.

Jim Smyth and David Cairns, in their contribution entitled 'Dividing loyalties: local identities in a global economy', contrast the impact of the forces of globalisation north and south of the border. Their views, trenchantly presented, emphasise the enthusiastic embracing of this process in the south, which can lead to a weakening of the nation-state, the imposition of a global culture and the dissolution of bonds of community and class. In the north, globalisation has marginalised a significant minority of Protestants. Their intense identification with loyalism is presented as a mani-festation of the resistance to this process. The authors point to the uneven nature of the process of globalisation: its effects depend on the ability and willingness of indigenous cultural forms to resist or embrace it.

Faced with a capitalist logic which more than ever functions on a global level, the Irish state has succeeded in generating the kind of energy, expertise and capital that in part overcame the dependency of Ireland on foreign investment. Seán Ó Riain, in 'Soft solutions to hard times' argues that the state has contributed in an important way to the emergence of an Irish-owned software sector, which is now a significant international player. Global flows have, in this context, amplified the impact of local initiatives onto the world-scene. They have facilitated the emergence of a new Irish capitalist class, technically sophisticated and able to thrive in the global economy.

Eamonn Slater, in 'When the *local* goes global', is concerned with how a local place, an Irish pub, has become part of the global flow of commodities and images. He investigates how this cultural identity becomes embedded in other global spaces, outside Ireland.

The ability of locales to use global processes for their own purposes is further illustrated by Ruth Casey. In 'Virtual locality', she looks at a particular community on the western seaboard of Ireland. This place is predominantly inhabited by residents who are not local. The revival of this declining community has squarely relied on these outsiders. Not only have they enhanced the local social life, but they have mobilised global networks in order to do so. The opportunities offered by globalisation have been exploited in order to regenerate the locality.

MEMORY AND IDENTITY

CHAPTER 1

Re-membering 1798

PADDY O'CARROLL

A Jewish proverb states that 'to remember is the secret of redemption'. In recent years we seem to have celebrated more than our usual quota of anniversaries of past events: 1916, the Great Famine, 1798 and the ending of World War I. Remembering is one of society's most important cultural processes. When we commemorate, we evoke the continuity of tradition. We are reassured by the fact that the past, having already happened, cannot be altered. But the past is claimed by various peoples; opposing groups defend their many different and even contradictory versions of the same past.

The invitation to commemorate usually comes from a dominant or potentially dominant group. It hopes to co-ordinate the interests of other groups through the creation of 'not only a unison of economic and political aims, but also *intellectual and moral unity*'.[1] Commemoration is primarily of interest, therefore, because of the role it plays in the struggle for domination. Of course, total co-ordination of interests is never possible. The never-ending struggle to appropriate and transform popular memory is, therefore, a

---

1 A. Gramsci, *Selections from the prison notebooks*, London: Lawrence and Wishart, 1971.

vital part of all politics. Collective remembering is a political act, an art form distinguished by 'selective retention, innocent amnesia and tendentious re-interpretation'.[2] Commemoration involves the co-ordination of the memories of different communities. The memory of 1798 was used in 1998 and throughout history in an attempt to appropriate and control popular memory.

Sponsors and patrons

The need felt by the state to be involved in the recent commemoration of 1798 probably resulted from its failure, in 1991, to commemorate the anniversary of the 1916 rising. This had left the field open to political opponents. The commemoration of 1798 could also prove useful in furthering the peace process. The state moved to mobilise its forces well in advance of the anniversary date. The Department of the Taoiseach set up Comoradh '98 to fund and manage the commemoration. The total budget was over £350,000. All public authorities were requested to inform the government of their plans for commemorating 1798. An official calendar of events was drawn up. Historians, the professional custodians of the public memory, were brought on side with research funds. Local authorities identified places where a monument or plaque might be erected. With some sensitivity, they liaised with individuals whose ancestors had been involved in the conflicts of 1798. The first important outcome of this intervention was a measure of co-option of local activists.

They endeavoured to depoliticise the commemoration by the use of a set of rhetorical techniques. For example, the declared official theme of Comoradh activities, 'Christian unity', tended to empty historical discourses of their local, concrete meanings. In a similar manner, a junior minister

---

2   J. Brow, 'Notes on community, hegemony and the uses of the past', *Anthropological Quarterly*, vol. 63, no. 1, 1990, p. 3.

described the rebellion of 1798 as 'non-sectarian, democratic and inspired by the French and American revolutions'.[3] In a process of 'idealisation', the past was cleaned up and made into the palatable embodiment of dominant values. Terms remarkably similar to those of the current peace process were used and the issues of sectarianism and insurrection were avoided.

This official view was brought to Wexford by a Comoradh seminar to advance understanding of the period of the rebellion; an objective not fully appreciated by some Wexford activists. A permanent site of official memory was established in the new Fr John Murphy Interpretative Centre in Boolavogue. The churches played their role in encouraging reconciliation with other denominations. The political edge was also blunted by the aesthetic style of officially chosen musical events. For instance, Mozart's *Requiem* was performed in Wexford, Dublin and Belfast by choirs from France, and the north and south of Ireland. Some of the commercial musical products also reflected the atmosphere of the polite drawing room or choral society more than that of the haunts of insurrectionists and their contemporary sympathisers.

Though the above steps led to a considerable degree of official control, it was not possible to prevent all embarrassing eventualities or to avoid a clash of symbolisms. For example, a minor imbroglio occurred at the unveiling of a plaque commemorating the hanging, by the British authorities, in Cork in 1797, of a number of soldiers for the administration of oaths within the ranks. By bizarre coincidence, the ceremony was conducted with the national flag at half-mast owing to the death of Diana Princess of Wales. Having protested for a short time, some of the participants left in disgust before the ceremony commenced, having labelled all and sundry as so-and-so 'Brits'.[4]

---

3 *The Echo*, 28 July 1997.
4 I wish to acknowledge this communication from a participant.

It is obvious from the above account that what was officially remembered from the past in 1998 was greatly influenced by the strategic interests of the sponsors. The broader picture of past commemorations of the events of 1798 illustrates that the 1798 celebrated in each case (1848, 1898 and 1948) was also an uncanny reflection of the very different social and political concerns of the dominant or potentially dominant groups. Some of the atmosphere of the fiftieth anniversary of 1798 can be deduced from John Kells Ingram's poem of the period, significantly entitled 'The Memory of the Dead'. Lines such as 'Who fears to speak of ninety eight?', and

> All, all are gone, but still live on
> The fame of those who died.
> But true men like you men
> Remember them with pride,

were a call from the radical Protestant sector of society for an end to half a century of enforced amnesia, during which the insurrection had been subjected to an official taboo.

In contrast, the tone of the centenary commemoration in 1898 was set mainly by the burgeoning nationalists who used the opportunity to pressurise the state for home rule. 1798 was reinterpreted largely in Catholic nationalist terms.

The next major anniversary in 1948 was very much an official state affair. It was conducted with military pomp and circumstance. The regime was inward looking and interested mainly in consolidating its own power. The historical international dimension, such as the role of France and the United States, received scant recognition.

The above brief survey is sufficient to indicate that these celebrations evoked very different interpretations. 1798 was, at different times, mobilised in support of state reform, revolt against the regime in power, and finally in support of the new regime. The appeal was made by, successively, the Protestant middle class, the Catholic elites seeking independence, and finally the ruling regime of the new Irish state.

Contesting memories

In 1998, various groups resisted this co-ordination and asserted their own narratives. Memory or rather memories are socially constructed. Knowledge of the past constitutes a major part of identity and consciousness and it is inevitable that many groups resist incorporation into the intellectual and moral ethos of the state. We examine two significant groups who resisted the co-ordination of their memory: first, communities in a locality associated with the rebellion, and second, Sinn Féin.

It should be remembered that the public celebrated 1798 over a period of 124 years before the foundation of the present state. The memory of the most cataclysmic civil strife in the history of the country, one that cost 30,000 lives, remained very much alive for a long time, not only in folklore and popular ballads, but also in literature. In particular, the 1898 celebrations had revived the narrative for many. This tradition was also enhanced in the run up to 1998, as a new set of social relations based on co-operation and friendship, including even a network on the Internet, arose between guardians of local sites, local historians, groups of battle enactors, political groups, and the churches. Of course, they negotiated and fought for their interpretation and its associated ideals. The most secure in their identity were the members of localities associated with the events of 1798. They possessed a living memory, an unbroken folk tradition, and so had least need of official commemoration. Their case illustrates well the pitfalls involved in state-sponsored commemoration.

Perhaps the highest level of resentment provoked by the official celebrations occurred in such localities. Locals felt that the state and their academic experts had failed to acknowledge that the role of such localities in the events of 1798 placed them closest of all to the heroes of 1798. A Wexford councillor expressed very well the chagrin generated by the discrepancies between locals' memories of 1798 and the distortions of the official discourse. He characterised the latter as 'half truths . . . for the pacification of certain elements involved in the power struggle in the occupied part of our country'. He further asserted the local view that 'the events of May and June 1798 were sectarian'; and then clarified that he was 'only protecting [his] heritage' against those who, with hard cash, 'were buying the souls of our martyrs'.[5]

The struggle of this Wexford representative for control over the interpretation of his past revolved around not only a unique local memory, but also ties of blood with original participants. The community felt it was almost their contemporary embodiment. They thus felt that their claims to primacy were well supported. Undoubtedly, the contrast with the official welcome for the relatives of Tone must have galled them. The perceived distortions of official discourse denied the truths of local memory to such an extent that common cause with the state under the symbol of 1798 was unthinkable.

In contrast, the approach of Sinn Féin was more instrumental, as it arose from an oppositional form of memory. When Gerry Adams arrived at Vinegar Hill in February 1998, accompanied by a colour party dressed in black and a contingent of local pikemen, his narrative of 1798 was, surprisingly, largely indistinguishable from the official version, indicating Sinn Féin's new role in constitutional politics. In emphasising, however, that the revolution of 1798 was 'unfinished', as the tie with Britain was unbroken, Sinn Féin reverted to its more usual oppositional form. The continuity between 1798 and the present was emphasised by the presentation of a golden pike to Adams by local pikemen; the Sinn Féin poster of the event also depicted both Wolfe Tone and a local man, recently killed on active service in London. The Comoradh response was to state that the pikemen involved 'had nothing whatever to do with the Comoradh'.[6]

---

5 *The Echo,* 28 August 1997.
6 *The Echo,* 26 February 1998.

The above account of different approaches to the celebration of 1798 illustrates how history is turned into legend
and how hopes and desires become 'truth', reminding us of
Renan's assertion that 'forgetting . . . and historical error are
an essential factor in the creation of a nation'.[7] The recent
commemoration of 1798 was based on an amalgam of three
historical types of memory. First, we have identified a folk
memory, such as that in County Wexford, in which the
physical fabric of the local community, every named field,
battle site and hero's birthplace, are monuments to the past.
Collective memory is sustained in the thousand and one
minor rituals that characterise everyday life. The second,
and most predominant, type of memory is that cultivated by
new large states wishing to assert their distinct boundaries.
They use commemorations and public monuments in the
attempt to foster an identity more in tune with the economic
and political developments of the time. Both the 1898 and
1948 commemorations borrowed this style of state ritual.

However, collective memory is beginning to change under
the influence of the major social forces that are transforming
societies everywhere. In the 1998 commemoration we have
noticed a third type of memory shaped by the forces of
democratisation, with greater participation by the ordinary
citizen, and of commercialisation, represented by the sale of
badges, t-shirts and music and by the heritage industry. In
fact the latter now tends to perform the function played by
monuments in the past. Finally, in the research, seminars
and contributions of experts to public debate, we see the
influence of growing rationality.

Commemoration and the public sphere

The power of the popular past is derived precisely from the
fact that it is rudimentary, selective, based on simple
historical labels, focused on contemporary ideals and full of

---

7 E. Renan, 'What is a nation?', in S. Wolf (ed.), *Nationalism in
   Europe. 1815 to the present*, London: Routledge, 1996, p. 50.

retrospective inferences.[8] The 1798 or 1916 commemorated is a symbol in which we can condense a plethora of complex ideas, ideals and values and assert their importance and superior worth. When the past is recollected, our narratives are reconstructed to reinforce our identities and ideologies and to guide our interactions.[9] Popular culture requires simple but strongly contrasting categories in order to develop clear-cut identities. The words of Ingram's poem clearly contrast 'true men like you men' with 'cowards who mock the patriot's fate'. Commemorations seek to harness this energy.

However, as the above account demonstrates, commemoration may be a two-edged sword for patrons. First, the cultural forms in which memory is embedded, such as family and locality, possess a degree of autonomy. Hegemonic discourses can be disrupted, criticised and subjected to reversal. Second, the process of remembering is highly symbolic, a matter for interpretation. It is, therefore, open-ended, bounded only by the capacity of the communities to imagine. There cannot be a catechism of memory. Finally, the carnival aspect of celebration is poised between affirmation and rejection of the established order. All these tendencies diminish the state's capacity to create the desired remembrance. While the narrative aspect of commemoration satisfies fundamental needs by creating, symbolising and objectifying reality in a manner which enables experience to be endowed with meaning, it is also the basis of its less visible ideological powers.

The above struggles show that, as classical sociologists recognised, we can be either chained or liberated by the past. Durkheim and Halbwachs associated some of the ills of modern societies with the failure to remember.[10] In contrast,

8   P. Connerton, *How societies remember*, Cambridge: Cambridge University Press, 1989.

9   A. Cohen, *Masquerade politics*, Oxford: Oxford University Press, 1993.

10 E. Durkheim, *The division of labour in society*, New York: The Free Press, 1964; M. Halbwachs, *The collective memory*, New York: Harper Colophon, 1980.

modernists have perceived the appeal to the past as equally pathological, a 'false consciousness' that clouds reality. Both points of view are important.

1798 has been used to instigate a variety of public spheres. When we contrast the commemorations in 1948 and 1998 we can see considerable change. The triumphalist focus on the heroic past in 1948 created an image of an agonistic public sphere, depending on an enlightened leader, regime-oriented, conformist, narrow, exclusive and inward-looking. Such was the conformity, that one commentator subsequently described the regime's leadership style as 'the plying of sleeping dogs with tranquillisers'.[11] This style has also been described as making the polity 'drunk on remembrance'.[12]

The commemoration in 1998 has shifted the public sphere in a somewhat more emancipatory direction, which may herald greater flexibility and freedom in politics generally. Recent commemorations have signalled a re-awakening of interest in the use of the past. The continuing displacement of the nationalist and traditional culture has been halted for the present. Rapid modernisation brings change and disruption, but modernity lacks the capacity to re-imagine community. Its criticism of narrow ideologies is welcome, but it needs to be superseded in the interests of emancipation. The 1998 commemorations carried with them an emancipatory and utopian element. 1798 has shown us a past that is essential to the formation of an acceptable, balanced modernity. In this sense, our commemoration of 1798 can be said to have contributed somewhat to a reformulation of our identity, a re-membering as it were, which hopefully carries within it the seeds of our political redemption.

---

11 F. Shaw, 'The canon of Irish history – A challenge', *Studies*, LXI, no. 242, 1972.
12 F. Fanon, *The wretched of the earth*, Harmondsworth: Penguin, 1967.

STANDS TO THE MEMORY OF

...ERS AND SISTERS WHO PERISHED

...THE HOLOCAUST.

CHAPTER 2

Technologies of Memory

FARREL CORCORAN

The traditional academic approach to memory has been to analyse it as a mental faculty of individuals, doing its work in isolation from any social or historical context. With the revival of interest in the work of Maurice Halbwachs, however, scholarly emphasis is now firmly on memory as an inherently social activity, a major link between individual social behaviour and cultural forces operating over time.[1] An individual's memory can now be seen as the unique product of a particular intersection of group memories.

Communication plays a central role in this. A family remembering the past with the help of the photo album demonstrates how memory is subject to on-the-spot selections and revisions, through which the identity of the family is established. On a somewhat larger sociological scale, the process of public commemoration embodied in loyalist street culture in Northern Ireland provides a cultural framework in which children and adults alike learn in ritualised ways what to remember and what to forget about the past in Ireland. Various symbolic practices – graffiti, kerb painting, dress codes, traditional emblems, William of Orange murals,

---

1 M. Halbwachs, *On collective memory,* Chicago: University of Chicago Press, 1992.

band parades, bonfires, the thundering of Lambeg drums and the shrieking of flutes – function to reconstruct shared memories and to silence alternative versions of the past.

Memory, and amnesia, plays an immense social role in constituting groups in the present, in telling us who we are, embedding our present selves in our past. Social identities are held together by a common stock of memories constructed, sustained, learned, inherited and transmitted by families, clubs, street gangs, rural co-operatives, churches, ethnic groups and nation-states. In an important sense, real communities are communities of memory, capable of sustaining a context of meaning for their members that orients them towards the future. Memory is one of the major components of social identity and also one of the clearest guides to its configuration. Any analysis of social identity and consciousness becomes an analysis of group perceptions of the past, because the way memories are generated and understood by social groups is a direct guide to how they understand their position in the present. Cultural memory is an active, absorbing, inventive social practice of creating meaning by engaging with the past. Cultural amnesia can be seen as the generation of memory in new forms, in a continuing process of interpretation of the past. Memory is therefore a narrative to be analysed for what it can tell us about how the past affects the present, rather than a replica of a true experience that can be retrieved and relived.

In Ireland, debates about revisionism among professional historians and their popularisers in the press highlight the institutional aspect of the social organisation of remembering and forgetting. They point to the role of universities, newspapers, publishing houses and archives, and stress the fact that recovering the truth of the past is often an ideological enterprise influenced by current political tensions; in this case how we deal with the end of the British colonial project in Ireland.

Technologies of memory

Remembering together is primarily achieved within the practices of ordinary conversation, which support shared ways of describing key events and shared criteria for evaluating those descriptions. British discourse about the royal family recapitulates ordinary citizens' awareness of their social position in British society in relation to a family that is given special status.[2] Irish discourse about GAA sports confirms county identity within a larger narrative expressing popular national sentiment and Irish ethnic distinctiveness. Communal identities are lived out in language and social relations, but the electronic media play a role too as they co-opt the narrative patterns of conversational discourse: the well-told anecdote, the flow of gossip, the crafted joke, the nostalgic intonation of reminiscence, that owe more to oral tradition than to the literate heritage of the newspaper. The arrival of radio in Ireland made it possible to summon into being the aural representation of the imagined community in which sporting activities are constructed into symbolic national events.[3] It eroded spatial distance, allowing scattered audiences to be transported in imagination to other parts of the country and to be incorporated continually into the elaboration of a common national memory, at the same time as identities were being strengthened around parish, county and province. Great games and great players became ingrained in the national psyche. *Seamus?*

It is in this context that Marita Sturken, borrowing from Foucault, refers to the media as 'technologies of memory', because they both embody and generate cultural memory.[4]

---

2 M. Billig, 'Collective memory, ideology and the British Royal Family', in D. Middleton and E. Derel (eds.), *Collective remembering*, London: Sage, 1991.

3 B. Anderson, *Imagined communities. Reflections on the origins and spread of nationalism,* London: Verso, 1983.

4 M. Sturken, *Tangled memories: The Vietnam War, the AIDS epidemic and the politics of remembering,* Berkeley: University of California Press, 1997.

They are also implicated in the power play of memory production, as sites in which struggle for competing forms of remembering and forgetting takes place. The memorial is the most traditional form of memory technology, but new forms are being generated in the heritage industry (the interactive heritage centre) and even in commodity culture (ribbons, buttons, posters, coffee mugs and t-shirts).

The camera constitutes probably the most significant technology of memory in the contemporary world, as its images feed into photography, cinema and television. Visual media address us with the illusion of pure immediacy and presence, obscuring the fact that the past is not just there in memory, it has to become articulated through technology before it becomes memory. Television, for instance, is not a vessel in which peoples' memories passively reside, but a technology that, using well-established ideological and pro-duction codes, selects and organises images, sounds, voices, landscapes, text, colours and motion into new patterns. Through the application of technology by particular social agents, memories are produced, shared and given new meaning.

Unity and difference

We now turn to investigate the workings of cultural memory and amnesia in the process of cultural negotiation posed by recent flows of immigration into Ireland. Culturally organised remembering and forgetting is ideological to the extent that shared images of the past function as important forces in the constitution of in-group/out-group identities in the present. The Irish experience of recent flows of migration into and across western Europe reflects some of the major changes taking place in Irish culture in this period of late modernity. These are linked to the declining strength of the traditional sources of identity (such as religion, workplace, family and nation) that sustained particular structures of collective memory before now. They are also linked to the increasing power of the print and broadcast media to produce and reinforce emotionally charged notions of collective identity, including people's sense of racial, ethnic, gender and class difference, and to establish a common-sense consensus.

Subtle cultural adjustments to new patterns of mass human dislocation and migration are taking place in all western European countries. However, the Irish situation is uniquely influenced by the winding down of 'the Troubles' and the search for political initiatives designed finally to deal with the legacy of the colonial past in Northern Ireland. This involves extensive public debate scrutinising as never before what it now means to be Irish or British, nationalist or loyalist. This debate is paralleled by a no less robust debate on extending citizenship, in a more open Ireland, to refugees and asylum seekers. As citizenship and cultural identity are highlighted in new constitutional formulations in the so-called Good Friday Agreement, inherited structures of feeling, making national identity co-terminus with ethnicity and territory, are being scrutinised as never before in the public sphere.

Given the general public perception that we are a generous people, committed to higher than average financial contributions to overseas development programmes and disaster relief funds, how open can we expect Ireland to be to inward migration, particularly to those displaced by civil turmoil in Africa and eastern Europe? A European Commission survey of attitudes in 1997, commissioned as part of the European Year Against Racism, provides some insight into comparative levels of racism in Europe. Fifty-five per cent of Irish respondents described themselves as 'racist' but only 9 per cent agreed with the statement: 'I favour unconditional repatriation of all immigrants and their children, legal and illegal' (the European average was 65 per cent and 20 per cent respectively). Racist attitudes right across Europe correlated strongly with dissatisfaction with people's life circumstances, fear of unemployment, insecurity about the future and lack of confidence in the political system; these feelings are associated in particular with the old, the unemp‍l and unskilled workers. Disparities between Iris‍

European countries' attitudes might be expected when we compare differences in actual experiences of immigration. While Ireland has been an exporter of people for many years and had minimal experience of immigration prior to the 1990s, many of our European neighbours have known immigration since the mid-twentieth century. By the early 1970s, for example, one-seventh of all manual workers in Germany and the UK were immigrants and in France, Belgium and Switzerland immigrants made up one-quarter of the industrial workforce.

Viewed out of context, the increase in numbers seeking asylum in Ireland seems startling and indeed has been used by some politicians and anti-immigration campaigners to ignite a moral panic about a small country being 'overwhelmed' by a 'tidal wave' of asylum seekers. In 1992, thirty-nine people applied for asylum and fourteen were approved. In 1997, 3,800 applied and 332 were approved. In 1998, there were 4,600 asylum applications. These figures are tiny by international comparisons: while Ireland had a backlog of 6,500 applications at the end of 1998, the UK alone had a waiting list of 52,000. Ireland receives only one out of every hundred asylum applications filed in Europe and rejects 90 per cent of those.

Media performance

How is the actual migration phenomenon behind these statistics being mediated to Irish people who have no direct experience of it? Refugee-related issues can be found on the Irish media agenda only in recent years and the spread of opinion is similar to that found in other western European countries. The tabloid press veers periodically towards inciting moral panics with headlines which go far beyond the content of their stories ('Refugee Rapist on the Rampage', 'Refugee Gang Bust', 'Refugees Housed in Top Dublin Hotels'). Although tabloid headlines are designed to be eye-catching rather than to sum up accurately the theme of the story, they nevertheless play a significant role in processing

30

information. A biased representation of refugees is less obvious in the broadsheet press, but analysis of its discourse reveals linguistic subtleties that corroborate many of Teun Van Dijk's conclusions about racism and the press elsewhere.[5]

It is very normal to find refugees discursively positioned as helpless people leading joyless lives and passively depending on state institutions. Rarely are they seen as active agents who speak up for themselves and rarely are they referred to as potential contributors to Irish society, as professionals or employment providers. Seldom is there reference to the above-average scholastic achievement of immigrant children in other countries, driven by the ambition of parents with a hunger for accumulating socially useful intellectual capital.

Broadcasting, with its ideology of immediacy and its roots in oral tradition, probably has more potential than newspapers to provide a public forum in which identity issues related to migration can be included in the debate about citizenship and nationality. One such forum was created in December 1997 when RTÉ, responding to its public service mandate, decided on a blitz approach to consciousness raising. It scheduled, over three consecutive nights, several documentaries and studio discussions on different aspects of refugees and multiculturalism, heralded to viewers beforehand as exceptional programming and with an on-screen introduction by former president, Mary Robinson.

In this concentration of primetime themed programming on the national television station, we can discern the clear lines of a technology of memory deployed in a deliberate way to intervene in the debate about Irish identity and implicitly promote tolerance of ethnic difference. The documentary *Operation Shamrock* explored identity from the point of view of German children who had come to Ireland in 1946 as war refugees, and who were now Irish citizens. It used the narrative format of quest to explore their contemporary

---

5 T. Van Dijk, *Racism and the press,* London: Routledge, 1991.

search for their German roots and the circumstances of their adoption. In the interstices between the individuals' stories, some of them happily Irish, some feeling robbed of their true identities, ethnocentric notions of what it means to be Irish were implicitly stretched.

Louis Lentin's documentary *No More Blooms* was less reticent in setting out the cruel context of the arrival of these five hundred refugee children in Ireland. With Jewish refugees from fascism in the 1930s and 1940s seeking shelter wherever they could, in Ireland they found very little comfort. A mixture of anti-Semitism and self-interest coalesced to keep out Jews and other 'undesirables' from an Ireland that saw itself as a country of emigration, not immigration. Fear of Jews coming in to take over Irish trade was as strong as it was in other parts of Europe. Government documents recently released from the National Archives, dramatised in reconstructions and juxtaposed with Nazi film of mass killings and deportations, highlighted an official reluctance to throw open doors to the persecuted of Europe unless they could have a positive impact on employment in Ireland. The Irish ambassador in Berlin, Charles Bewley, deflected requests for visas with a stream of anti-Semitic rhetoric, directed back towards Dublin, which echoed Nazi propaganda closely.

Lentin's revisionist television intervention worked to change the contemporary dominant memory of the Holocaust, in which it was largely assumed Ireland played no part. This temporal linking of the 1930s with the 1990s was taken one step further with the spatial juxtaposition of Ireland's current official reluctance to accept refugees with an innovative refugee programme being implemented in Liberia under economic conditions incomparably worse than those prevailing in Ireland. The documentary was the dominant form favoured throughout the week, but vox pop technique and live studio discussion were also utilised to examine current refugee problems and the rise of racism in many parts of Irish society.

As a technology of memory, this themed programming worked on its audiences to puncture the common sense of sedimented identity feelings that would construe Irish hospitality as a central feature of the national character. The codes and narrative styles (stressing personal explorations of identity and memory, expanding the notion of adoption in ways that did not exclude the emotional, translating archival material into dramatisations) used by television enabled audiences to respond with empathy and involvement. Preferred memories of World War II, inherited from an older generation, were given a new framing as partial and biased accounts that excluded Irish awareness of the Nazi genocide project being rolled out on mainland Europe. Memories that had been screened out for a long time were drawn back into focus, as television selected new images and voices and arranged them in unfamiliar ways. Not only was all this available to the large television audience it attracted, but it was vigorously promoted by RTÉ and given further amplification through previews, reviews, interviews, still photos and full news articles that appeared in all daily, evening and Sunday newspapers, as well as several provincial papers and on local radio. Many of the themes were explored still further in the main RTÉ Radio current affairs programmes.

Conclusion

Irish print and electronic media are intensively involved in the reshaping of cultural identities in the way they structure popular discourses to articulate the memories and meanings that are associated with particular identities. The instability of memory and the role of mediated discourse via radio or television as technologies of memory can be seen very clearly in the Irish response to recent immigration patterns. It is clear in retrospect that the ideological conflict embedded in the debate about refugees in Ireland in the late 1990s displayed all the classic features of a moral panic, crystallising public anxiety and confusion about the nature of Irish identity. It triggered a sustained campaign against immigration, which appealed to people alarmed by an apparent breakdown of the social order that might leave them at

economically as well as culturally. For the refugees themselves, the effect of this moral panic was a rapid increase in
the level of hostility directed at them, both symbolic and
physical.

The most salient factor in the competing discourses of
memory and forgetting currently working their way through
popular culture is the overwhelming presence of emigration
in the Irish historical imagination. This is based on actual
population flows out of Ireland to North America, Australia
and the UK during the nineteenth and twentieth centuries
and on the huge presence in the Irish public consciousness
of its diaspora. Voices urging increased openness to the
emergence of a multicultural Ireland point to the contradictions inherent in the rhetoric of xenophobia and are
struggling to get a hearing in the media.

Whether these voices of our past are going to be heard
(and thereby remembered) or not (forgotten) remains to be
seen. Whatever happens in the future, one thing is certain:
the modern technologies of memory are going to play their
part in our culturally organised acts of remembering and
forgetting.

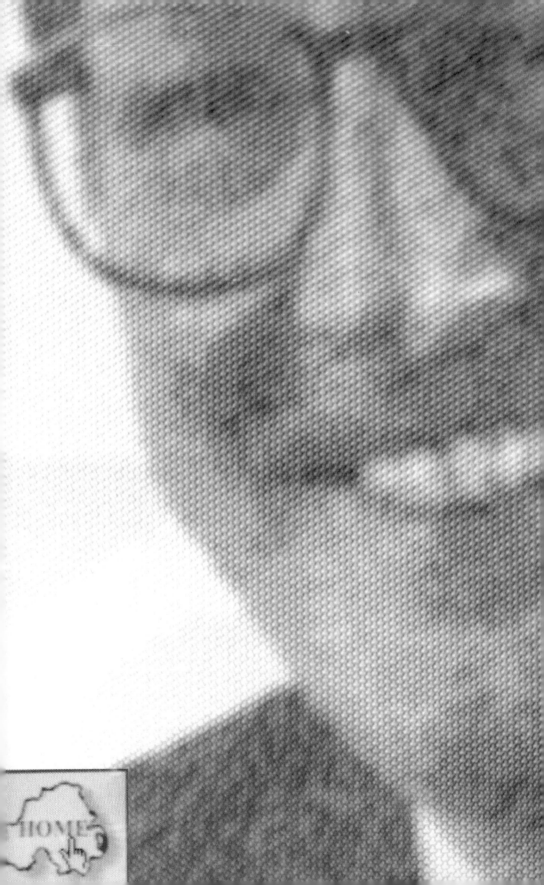

HOME

CHAPTER 3

The Orange Order of Things

COLIN COULTER

The ideological programme of Ulster unionism has traditionally rested upon the conviction that the Irish border marks the boundary between two fundamentally different forms of social order. In those texts that seek to advance the unionist cause, the UK invariably emerges as a model of the good society. Intellectuals and others within the unionist fold have increasingly sought to depict the Union as a form of political association founded upon the ideals of liberalism and pluralism. For instance, the prominent unionist thinker, Arthur Aughey, has consistently offered the view that the status of the UK as a multicultural society means that its public institutions are simply unable to garner legitimacy through appeals to particularistic identities such as ethnicity, religion and race.[1] In order to secure the allegiance of all of its diverse peoples, the British state is compelled as a matter of course to acknowledge those universal principles that find expression through the ideal of citizenship and the rule of law. Accordingly, the UK has assiduously assembled an extensive framework of

---

1 A. Aughey, 'The idea of the Union', in J. W. Foster (ed.), *The idea of the Union: Statements and critiques in favour of the Union of Great Britain and Northern Ireland*, Vancouver: Belcover, 1995, pp. 8–19.

legal protection that both underwrites the liberties of the individual and establishes an environment in which a diversity of ethnic and religious expression can flourish.

The essential modernity of the British state is considered to have given rise to an enduring material prosperity. The current generation of unionist intellectuals has striven consistently to portray the UK as one of the world's foremost economic powers. The operation of welfarist principles of redistribution on the part of the British state has led to increasingly generous subsidies being channelled into Northern Ireland. The existence of the annual subvention from Westminster has ensured, as unionists are at pains to point out, that public services and living standards in the six counties have tended to surpass those south of the border.

In unionist literature, the representation of the Irish Republic transpires, inevitably, to be rather less utopian. A central article of faith among unionist intellectuals has been that the course followed by the twenty-six counties since partition has offered offence to the liberal conscience. The architects of the Irish Republic are considered to have acted upon the assumption that there exists south of the border purely one people united in common allegiance to a shared ethno-religious heritage. The creation of a Gaelic Catholic orthodoxy throughout the twenty-six counties has infringed upon the rights both of the individual and of a series of minority groups. For the Ulster unionist, the quintessentially authoritarian and sectarian nature of the Irish Republic is evinced most readily in the steady decline of the Protestant community south of the border since partition.

The readings that are advanced within the unionist literature construct the Irish Republic as a place that is not only culturally retarded but also materially impoverished. Influential figures within the unionist fold have made much of the economic difficulties that have beset the twenty-six counties. In seeking to represent the underdevelopment of the Irish Republic, unionist ideologues have drawn heavily upon one of the essential signifiers of modernity – that of the road. The relative poverty of the infrastructure of southern

Ireland offers to many unionists compelling evidence of the wisdom of partition.

The divergent representations that unionists provide of the UK and Irish Republic feed directly into their understanding of the nature of the two principal ideological traditions that exist on the island. In the eyes of sympathetic intellectuals, unionism represents a political enterprise guided solely by reason. The allegiances that inform the unionist disposition are considered to arise purely out of a dispassionate judgement that the Union happens to be the most advantageous constitutional arrangement available. The ambition of the Ulster unionist to remain a British citizen is simply a desire to live in a prosperous and multicultural society that respects and protects the freedom of the individual.

Intellectuals aligned to the unionist cause evidently regard themselves as the custodians of an eminently rational ideological programme.[2] The conception of Irish nationalism which they possess turns out, however, to be somewhat less flattering. The political ambitions that animate Irish nationalists simply perplex unionist thinkers. In choosing or aspiring to live beyond the environs of the Union, the nationalist declares – from the unionist perspective – a preference for citizenship of a state that is both politically and economically underdeveloped. The ideological formation of Irish nationalism exists, therefore, beyond the pale of the rational. Indeed, within the unionist imagination the very existence of the Irish Republic proves emblematic of the triumph of emotion over reason.

New times

The relentlessly dystopian vision of the Republic of Ireland that unionist intellectuals typically advance frequently strains the credulity of the dispassionate viewer/reader/ listener. There are of course elements of the unionist reading

2   R. L. McCartney, 'They walk alone', *The Irish Times*, 26 June 1999.

that would have had at least a kernel of truth in the past. Certainly if one went back to the 1980s, the argument that the Republic of Ireland represents an economic casualty would appear reasonably persuasive. While the orthodox unionist perception of the twenty-six counties may have had some credibility in the past, this has been all but eroded by developments in recent years.

In the course of the 1990s, the Republic of Ireland has embarked upon a remarkable process of social change. The twenty-six counties have increasingly come to exhibit the essential hallmarks of a secular and liberal society. The scandals concerning the clerical abuse of children have both heralded and accelerated the decline of the power of the Catholic Church. As the moral authority of organised religion has waned, individuals have begun to explore alternative ways of being in the world. The current of pluralism that flows through contemporary southern Irish society has come to be acknowledged by the institutions of state. The Irish government has introduced a range of social legislation that promises to underwrite certain indispensable personal freedoms. Homosexuality has been legalised, contraceptives have become more freely available and the constitutional ban on divorce has been lifted. As the century turns, it would be difficult to name a single substantial civil liberty that the citizens of the UK enjoy that is denied to their counterparts in the Republic of Ireland.

The shifts that have occurred within the political culture of the Irish Republic have, significantly, entailed changes in attitudes towards the 'national question'. The 1990s would seem to have marked a dilution of certain versions of nationalist feeling within the twenty-six counties. It would of course be premature to pronounce the demise of orthodox nationalism within the Republic of Ireland. The ideal of Irish unification continues to exercise enormous appeal south of the border. Nonetheless, there have been signs over recent years that the citizens of the Irish Republic have come to adopt a rather less dogmatic approach towards Northern Ireland than was often the case hitherto. The growing pragmatism of people living in the twenty-six counties was evidenced most crucially perhaps in the enormous enthusiasm with which they greeted the Good Friday Agreement. The political deal envisaged that the Irish Constitution's claim on the six counties would be substantially revised and that in effect Northern Ireland would remain part of the UK for the foreseeable future. In choosing to endorse the Agreement so overwhelmingly, therefore, the voters of the Irish Republic revealed a willingness to dispense with some of the essential tenets of nationalist orthodoxy.

Perhaps the most significant developments that have overtaken contemporary southern Irish society have taken place within the economic field. In the 1980s, the Republic of Ireland appeared arrested in an especially dependent form of underdevelopment. The citizens of the twenty-six counties were burdened with proportionately greater public debt than those of any other state. The abiding frailty of the southern Irish economy, moreover, was indexed in the haemorrhage of mass emigration. The 1990s, however, would seem to have recorded a dramatic revival of the economic fortunes of the twenty-six counties. The Irish Republic has registered formal rates of economic growth that have clearly exceeded those of every other western European state. The seemingly phenomenal recent expansion of the southern Irish economy has of course inspired the formulation of the ubiquitous and increasingly tiresome metaphor of the Celtic Tiger.

The direction that the Irish Republic has taken in the course of the 1990s has undermined orthodox unionist constructions of the twenty-six counties. The literature of the late 1990s would suggest that the recent transformation of southern Irish society has drawn two rather different responses from unionist intellectuals. The first of these would seem to be the more prevalent.

Better the devil you know

Those pamphlets and articles that have appeared in the latter half of the 1990s indicate that there are elements within the unionist community that are currently in denial. Unionist intellectuals and others often appear unwilling and unable to acknowledge the scale and significance of the changes that have occurred south of the border during the 1990s. The anxiety of many unionists to cling to conventional readings of the Irish Republic has become especially apparent within contemporary economic debate.

The growth of the southern Irish economy has inevitably offered encouragement to the nationalist cause. Nationalists have counselled that the advent of the Celtic Tiger enhances the prospect that a thirty-two-county state would be financially viable. The contention that the economic conditions necessary for the unification of Ireland are currently materialising has of course invoked the ire of unionist intellectuals. Economists with unionist sympathies have begun to vigorously challenge the characterisation of the Irish Republic as the Celtic Tiger. In a trenchant and somewhat idiosyncratic pamphlet that appeared in 1997, the unionist academic and politician Esmond Birnie argued that the growth rates that have been declared within the twenty-six counties over the last few years have been inflated by the machiavellian practices of multinational corporations. The actual performance of the southern Irish economy, Birnie insists, lags considerably behind that suggested by the relevant official statistics. Rather than having undergone an economic miracle, the Irish Republic remains relatively underdeveloped and unable to keep the British citizens of Northern Ireland in the manner to which they have become accustomed. The material circumstances that would facilitate the unification of Ireland, therefore, still simply do not exist. The enterprise of Irish nationalism remains 'bad politics' guided by 'dubious economics'.

The interrogation of the Celtic Tiger that Birnie proffers often makes a good deal of sense. Indeed, elements of his critique can be found in the work of other economic commentators who are overtly hostile to the unionist project. The rational formalism of Birnie's prose cannot conceal, however, the particularism that informs his disposition. The purpose of a pamphlet such as *Without profit or prophets* is of course not merely to ascertain 'the truth' but also to advance specific ideological interests.[3] If the UK had registered growth rates comparable to those that have recently become the norm in the Irish Republic, it is difficult to imagine that a conservative like Esmond Birnie would subject the British economy to equally radical critique.

The writings of unionist intellectuals further reveal an unwillingness to recognise the seismic shifts that have occurred within the cultural and political life of the twenty-six counties during the 1990s. In the minds of many unionists, the Republic of Ireland continues to represent an essentially exclusive and authoritarian society. According to one member of the Cadogan Group – an alliance of unionist intellectuals – the Gaelic Catholic orthodoxy that reigned after partition has been 'modified only slightly' in recent times.[4] For many within the unionist community, the immutable nature of the Republic of Ireland finds especially insidious expression in the unflinching irredentism of the southern state. The seemingly substantial reformulation of nationalism that has taken place within the twenty-six counties over the last few years is often dismissed by unionists as purely cosmetic. The explicit acknowledgement of the principle of consent by successive Dublin administrations and the overwhelming support of the people of southern Ireland for the rewording of Articles 2 and 3 of the Irish Constitution are interpreted merely as astute strategic revisions. While the form of Irish republicanism may have altered, its substance remains unchanged. The ambition of the southern state to dominate and ultimately assimilate the six counties is unsated and indeed insatiable.

The marked unwillingness among unionist intellectuals to acknowledge the developments that have unfolded within southern Irish society over the previous generation clearly

3 E. Birnie, *Without profit or prophets: A response to businessmen and Bishops*, Belfast: Ulster Review Publication, 1997.
4 The Cadogan Group, *Rough trade: Negotiating a Northern Ireland settlement*, Belfast, 1998, p. 38.

undermines their claim to be the custodians of an entirely dispassionate and rational ideological tradition. Advocates of the Union have often claimed that their political allegiances are the outcome of an objective calculation of the relative merits of the various constitutional arrangements that are available. Unionist thinkers suggest that their opposition to the unification of Ireland reflects simply an aversion to living in a society that is sectarian and intolerant. The vision of the Irish Republic that has existed traditionally within the political imagination of Ulster unionism has always been somewhat tendentious. The representation of southern Ireland advanced by the present generation of unionist intellectuals, however, simply bears little resemblance to the realities of life today in the twenty-six counties. The construction of the 'other' within contemporary unionism would seem, therefore, to be the reflex of epistemological procedures rather different to those that would be conventionally understood as the exercise of reason. To have depicted the Republic of Ireland as an underdeveloped and authoritarian society two decades, or even one decade, ago would have had some credence. To rehearse the same argument today is merely to parade one's ignorance and prejudice for public perusal.

There's no place like home

The second unionist response to the recent trajectory of southern Irish society reveals a rather greater openness of mind. Over the last few years, some unionists have come to an understanding of the processes of revision at work south of the border. In a characteristically lucid essay commissioned by the Forum for Peace and Reconciliation, the leading unionist theorist Arthur Aughey delineates some of the liberal and secular currents that are presently redefining the twenty-six counties.[5] Aughey observes that the progressive trends

5 A. Aughey, 'Obstacles to reconciliation in the South', in *Building Trust in Ireland: Studies commissioned by the Forum for Peace and Reconciliation*, Dublin, 1996, pp. 1–52.

that may be discerned within contemporary southern Irish society are welcome in themselves. He moves on to contest that it would be naive, however, to expect that the liberal course followed by the twenty-six counties of late will have any real bearing upon the ideological disposition of the unionist community. The subtle argument that Aughey advances suggests that unionists are opposed to the nationalist enterprise not necessarily because they consider the Irish Republic to be culturally odious, but rather because they regard it as culturally 'different'. The island of Ireland simply does not constitute the site of the principal community to which members of the unionist tradition imagine themselves to belong. The particular path of development that the Irish Republic may pursue in the years to come will inevitably be unable, therefore, to convince unionists that their future lies outside the Union. Even the emergence within the twenty-six counties of a genuinely pluralist social formation that offered optimal civil liberties would be insufficient to persuade the unionist community to regard a united Ireland as home.

Aughey's essay reveals perhaps an important change of direction among the present generation of unionist intellectuals. Proponents of the unionist cause have, as we have seen, frequently argued that their constitutional preferences are simply an expression of rational calculation of interest. The unionist ambition to remain within the UK has been portrayed as being motivated primarily by a desire to live in a state that offers both enviable material prosperity and generous personal freedom. In the more recent writings of aligned intellectuals, however, we encounter an altogether less instrumental reading of the unionist mind. Those polemics that have appeared in the late 1990s have begun to advance an understanding of the unionist disposition as not only cerebral but, significantly, emotional also.

The likes of Arthur Aughey and John Wilson Foster have persisted with the view that unionism represents a pristine and dispassionate philosophical enterprise that orbits around the sacred and ultimately abstract ideal of citizenship. The recent work of these prominent figures has, however, come to reveal an appreciation that unionists are also animated by those substantive identities that give rise to feelings of kinship. The ideological project of unionism is held to rest upon not only a conviction that Westminster constitutes the birthplace of democracy but also a belief that the history of the six counties represents merely a subtext of the broader narrative of the UK. The constitutional affiliations of Ulster unionists are considered to articulate not only a sense that their fellow British citizens share an equally fervent devotion to the principles of liberal pluralism, but also a feeling that they share a common lineage with the peoples of England, Scotland and Wales. The inflection of contemporary unionist thought would appear, therefore, to be changing in subtle though significant ways. The most recent writings of certain sympathetic thinkers portray unionism less as an esoteric philosophical doctrine and more as a grounded way of being in the world.[6] It would seem, in other words, that unionist intellectuals are finally coming to terms with their own real status as the bearers of a version of British nationalism.

The shifts that have occurred recently within unionist discourse may be further read as a strategic response to the direction that southern Irish nationalism has taken since the mid-1980s. The increasingly substantial writings of unionist intellectuals evidently represent an attempt to secure ideological hegemony. The particular constructions that certain academics have advanced have clearly marked an ambition to establish unionism in a position of moral authority that would brook no challenge from Irish nationalism. Ironically, however, the counsel of the present generation of unionist intellectuals would seem often to have had precisely the opposite impact upon the nationalist tradition. Many within the nationalist fold have of course

6 For example, J. W. Foster, 'The task for Unionists', in J. W. Foster (ed.), *The idea of the Union: Statements and critiques in favour of the Union of Great Britain and Northern Ireland*, Vancouver: Belcover, 1995, pp. 69–74.

dismissed as mere cant the notion that unionism represents an abstract philosophical programme that centres upon the ideal of citizenship. Others would seem, however, to have taken rather more seriously the musings of thinkers committed to the unionist cause.

Elements within the twenty-six counties would appear to have believed for some time that the commitment of unionists to partition reflects an anxiety that the Republic of Ireland offers relatively few rights to the individual citizen. The creation of a unitary state on the island would require, therefore, the removal of those aspects of life south of the border that are offensive to the unionist conscience. This reformist zeal provided the inspiration of course for the ill-starred 'constitutional crusade' of the 1980s. In the 1990s, the ambition to render the Irish Republic more amenable to the unionist tradition has provided one of the multiple strands of the peace process. The recent endeavours of southern Irish nationalism to court the other principal ideological tradition on the island have encouraged unionism to change tack somewhat. Intellectuals and others have insisted that the revisions that are unfolding within the twenty-six counties are admirable but have no influence upon the political allegiance or sense of self of the unionist community. Unionists will remain opposed to a united Ireland, even a liberal pluralist one, precisely because it is a place that does not accord with their sense of historical or cultural self. Regardless of the renovations that are carried out, the Irish Republic remains a place that the Ulster unionist will never truly regard as home.

Conclusion

The constructions of the Republic of Ireland that unionists provide mercilessly expose the weakness of the ideological enterprise that they seek to advance. Intellectuals and others within the unionist community have consistently claimed that their aversion to the twenty-six counties has arisen out of a process of sober and reasonable reflection. The manner in which unionists have responded to the changes presently at work within southern Irish society has, however, revealed these claims to be distinctly threadbare. The inability of most unionist thinkers to come to terms with the liberal course that the Irish Republic has charted over the last generation suggests that they are animated by concerns that exist beyond the realm of pure reason. The shortcomings that it exhibits frequently move commentators to regard unionism as an antediluvian ideological formation. An alternative reading, however, suggests itself. Those who seek to promote the unionist cause frequently employ a discourse that emphasises the rational and universal in order to advance interests that are thoroughly unreasonable and particular. In so doing, unionists declare themselves the bearers of an ideological programme that is genuinely, and lamentably, modern.

CHAPTER 4

Reinventing Sinn Féin

AGNÈS MAILLOT

With the peace process and the IRA ceasefires, Sinn Féin has become a fashionable party, its leaders being given coverage on the airwaves and the credibility that they had been denied for years. Yet it is precisely because of the nature of Sinn Féin's involvement in the political arena over the last few years, and the changes the party has introduced not only to its language and strategies but also to its image, that republicans are now making inroads into Irish political circles. In the absence of the IRA, what is left of republican identity? With a mixture of activism and conciliation, Sinn Féin leaders have opted for respectability, while cultivating their working-class roots and claiming a historical line which they have, nevertheless, broken. Assisted by people like Martin McGuinness, Bairbre de Brún or Mitchell McLaughlin, Gerry Adams epitomises the new image of his party: that of *New Sinn Féin*, whose main objective is now to establish its credibility in order to remain a key player in the peace process and to consolidate its place in the Republic.

Edward Said, having in mind his native Palestine, pointed out the risky dialectic of the nationalist struggle for independence and socialist striving for liberation:

It's the tragedy, the irony, the paradox of all anti-imperialist or decolonising struggles that independence is the stage through which you must try to pass ... Therefore, the question for me is: how much of a price are we going to pay for this independence – if we can get it at all – and how many of the goals of liberation will we abandon?[1]

Even more critical is the time when independence can no longer be construed as the road to liberation. When this happens, all participants face the necessity of redefining themselves. Sinn Féin finds itself at such a critical juncture.

The politics of imaging

Maybe the most noticeable indicator of Sinn Féin's metamorphosis is the way it is now portrayed in the media. Whereas, for a long time, armed struggle dictated what should be in the news headlines, its cessation has opened many doors to republican leaders. Don Doyle, Sinn Féin's press officer in Dublin, admits that 'the ceasefire has created a more open climate'.[2] The repeal of the censorship laws in force until 1994 in Ireland and Britain, which prohibited the broadcasting of interviews and statements from republican spokespersons, has indeed greatly contributed to giving Sinn Féin access to the media. Sinn Féin has become news in itself, and few other party leaders in Ireland can boast the international media coverage that Adams gets on occasions. Thus, on 30 May 1996, the day of the Northern Ireland Forum election, there were no less than thirteen television camera crews and some seventy journalists outside the gate of an Andersonstown school to witness Gerry Adams' arrival.

The popularity that republicans seem to enjoy with the media is partly due to the fact that Sinn Féin cultivates a

---

1 M. Sprinkler, *Edward Said. A critical reader*, Oxford: Blackwell, 1992, pp. 236–7.
2 Interview with author, December 1998.

mixture of respectability and unconventionalism. Throughout the years Sinn Féin has learned not only how to steal the limelight but also how to remain in it. The art of communication is one of Sinn Féin's main assets. Republicans are keenly aware that the media can be used to their advantage, even, and chiefly, when the odds are against them. When it was about to be expelled from the talks in February 1998, as a result of an assassination which the RUC blamed on the IRA, Sinn Féin was at the heart of a week of suspense and drama which it had greatly contributed to orchestrating by multiplying statements and by threatening legal action against the government.

The importance that Sinn Féin gives to the media – one would once have spoken of propaganda – is not a new phenomenon. One of the first initiatives that the then Provisional Sinn Féin took after the 1970 split was to put in place two weekly newspapers in order to fill the gaps and to counter the bias that was, according to them, an inevitable feature of the establishment media. They also set up an efficient press office which produced countless statements and press releases. In 1999, Sinn Féin had eight press officers in Belfast, Dublin and Derry. Trained on the job, they had until recently to double their efforts to ensure that the name of the party would appear in the news, and have acquired the qualities essential to a good public relations policy: courtesy and availability. These lay press officers give their services for free, which contributes to lending a greater authenticity to their voices. According to media consultant Pat Montague, they can convey:

> . . . a clear sense of their own political strategy. They have a sense of confidence and of self-belief, they know exactly where they're going, they're clear on who their audiences are, which gives them an edge over other political parties. Sinn Féin are confident about their mission, and this is a key skill in terms of communications.[3]

---

3   Interview with author, December 1998.

But Sinn Féin's newly found success with the media would not have been possible had the party not refined its message. Long gone is the era of the simplistic discourse based on slogans such as 'Brits out', 'Victory to the IRA' and 'Down with the institutions of partition'. Sinn Féin presents itself as a reasonable party, which seeks to do everything possible in order for the institutions to work. Once banished from its repertoire, the very word 'institution' is nowadays frequently used by Sinn Féin's president, who has repeatedly stressed that his party will play the game, that it wants 'to turn the new institutions into power houses that will shape a new future for all the people of this island'.[4] This is quite different from the scathing discourse of the 1970s and 1980s, when the institutions were considered the very source of the conflict. During those decades, Sinn Féin was, in principle, opposed to any solution that would envisage an 'internal' settlement, not only deeming the Northern Ireland state illegitimate, but refusing to consider any solution in which the British government would retain some control over the province. One of the main objectives of the IRA campaign in the 1970s was precisely to make Northern Ireland ungovernable. Obviously, the Good Friday Agreement has enshrined new types of institutions, and Sinn Féin has carefully chosen its words to establish a marked difference between those and the 'institutions of partition'. 'This is no Stormont. The partitionist set-up of the past cannot be applied any longer', stressed Ard Comhairle member Martin Ferris during the extraordinary Ard Fheis in May 1998.[5]

Similarly, while for a long time Sinn Féin disparaged any solution negotiated with the help of the British, it is now ready to give an unprecedented endorsement to a British administration, deeming Tony Blair's government qualitatively different from all its predecessors. Sinn Féin goes even further, recognising, for the first time in its history, an

---

4   *The Irish Times*, 6 May 1998.
5   *The Irish Times*, 6 May 1998.

ally in the person of the British premier who can, according to Adams, become 'the British Prime Minister who can change Anglo-Irish relations, and to the mutual benefit of the people of these islands'.[6]

Entering mainstream politics and reaching the margins

But Sinn Féin still claims to be different, and in order not to be accused of compromising, and even betraying, its republican heritage, it has replaced the defence of principles that were once set in stone by a discourse in which it attributes to the party the safeguard and the future of the peace process. Mitchell McLaughlin does not mince his words when he stresses that 'Peace in Ireland will be achieved when the political parties can agree and form a government of national consensus. Sinn Féin's mission is to point the way'.[7] But the party has to be on its guard, for if the constitutional position has opened the doors of what Sinn Féin calls the 'establishment', that is, mainstream politics and the media, it could by the same token make Sinn Féin a superfluous party. It must thus retain its radical image and ensure that it has the political and strategic means of its new identity. Before the ceasefire, the guarantee of its difference could be summed up in three words: Irish Republican Army. But once orphaned of its armed wing, it has had to take its distances both from the moderate nationalism epitomised, in its view, by the SDLP and from the more extreme republicanism that is now embodied by armed dissident groups or by Republican Sinn Féin. These organisations' struggle is deemed outmoded, and even anachronistic. Nevertheless, the language of Ruairí Ó Brádaigh is not very different from that which Sinn Féin used until recently. Indeed, when this militant from the old

6 Sinn Féin Press Release, *Address by Sinn Féin President Gerry Adams MP to the Institute of Directors*, 26 November 1998.
7 M. McLaughlin, 'The Irish Republican ideal', in N. Porter (ed.), *The Republican ideal: Current perspectives*, Belfast: Blackstaff Press, 1998, p. 74.

guard justifies armed struggle by the following axiom: 'Resistance to British rule is a fact of life',[8] one only has to recall how republican leaders legitimised the IRA's actions.

For the first time in its history, Sinn Féin has unambiguously condemned an attack committed in the name of a united and republican Ireland, that of Omagh in August 1998. The words of Gerry Adams were harsh: 'I am totally horrified by this action and I condemn it without any equivocation whatsoever'.[9] Indeed, the revulsion caused by this massacre, whether political or moral, could only lead to strong condemnation. Obviously this attack went against the strategy put in place by the republican movement since the early 1990s, and any prevarication would have undoubtedly undermined its credibility as a defender of peace. But Omagh was not the only so-called blunder from a republican organisation, even though it was the bloodiest in the history of the conflict. Hearing republicans adopt the language of those who for decades castigated the IRA can nevertheless seem surprising, considering that Sinn Féin has repeatedly stated its refusal to enter the media battle of condemnation. The harsh words of Sinn Féin's president, like those of Martin McGuinness, signalled a turning point in republican thinking, while pointing to a greater confidence in the party as a political machine. Sinn Féin now seems ready to admit that it no longer needs the IRA to justify its struggle, that armed struggle is no longer a necessary guarantee of its republican pedigree. Since August 1998, Sinn Féin has entered the mainstream of Irish politics.

Sinn Féin must now find a place and a role to play in the new Irish order that has come about as a result of the Agreement. It is clear that its peaceful strategy brings some electoral dividends. The party substantially improved its electoral results in the last British general election, going from 10 per cent of the vote in 1992 to 16 per cent in May

---

8   *The Irish Times*, 6 May 1998.
9   *The Irish Times*, 17 August 1998.

1997, and winning two seats. But its electoral rise might have reached its peak in the north. In order to increase its representation, Sinn Féin would have to win some votes from the SDLP, whose vote, incidentally, increased in much less dramatic proportions, going from 23.55 per cent to 24 per cent. One of Sinn Féin's priorities is thus to make a visible breakthrough in the Republic, but in order to do so, it must free itself from the single-issue-party straitjacket in which it has greatly contributed to confining itself. Sinn Féin can count on several assets. It is a young party, which attracts enthusiastic recruits. Its leader is unanimously accepted within its ranks, and his popularity, in Ireland as well as abroad, is beyond doubt. Finally, Sinn Féin is an ambitious party, which describes itself as 'the fastest growing party in Ireland', and which can show initiative.[10] It aims to become the only authentic socialist party of the island and to impose itself as a radical force. Sinn Féin claims to be, in its own words, 'the party of the people of no property throughout this island'.[11] The electorate that it seeks to attract as a priority includes the most disadvantaged categories of the population, and its work on the ground, as in the most neglected districts of urban areas such as Tallaght, has been quite successful. It is in this type of environment that Sinn Féin can hope to maximise its representation.

The party claims to be socialist, but its tactics are also populist in nature, since parliamentary action is not, according to Don Doyle, the only field of action open to Sinn Féin. Inspired by tactics inherited from the strong methods of the IRA, republican politicians tackle the problems head on, as in the Dublin districts severely hit by the drugs problem. At the height of the drugs crisis in 1996, gardaí suspected republican involvement in groups such as Concerned Parents against Drugs. Although this in itself was

---

10 Sinn Féin Ard Comhairle, *Political report to the Ard Fheis*, www.sinnfein.ie.
11 *The Irish Times*, 22 May 1998.

not reprehensible, the methods used by suspected IRA members would tend to cast a shadow over Sinn Féin's democratic commitment. Similarly, the punishment beatings in Northern Ireland are still a major obstacle on the road to respectability. Sinn Féin is quite uncomfortable with this type of practice. Adams explained, during the Forum election campaign in May 1996, that 'the people of these areas want to be policed. They are law-abiding citizens. They should not be subject to the anti-social behaviour of a small group of malcontents. Punishment beatings, so-called, are very imperfect. Sinn Féin is opposed to those'.[12] But the party does not seem to be capable of putting an end to this type of action. According to RUC statistics on paramilitary attacks, which combine beatings and shootings, republicans were responsible for 93 such attacks in 1998, compared to 194 in 1997 and 175 in 1996. Obviously, punishment beatings do not solely occur on the republican side. The number of attacks by loyalist paramilitaries was: 123 in 1998 and 124 in 1997.[13]

Electoral strategies

It is on this point that Sinn Féin is most vulnerable in the Republic. It is not clear whether the Irish electorate will endorse or condone the militia-like tactics of the party, or of those claiming to act on behalf of republicans. And here lies one of the most difficult contradictions that the party has to overcome. Although it has entered the political mainstream, it refuses to be a mainstream party. It bases its future on difference, while seeking a vote that is not merely a protest one, as was the case in many instances until recently. Its ambition is to become a force with which the future political leaders of the country will have to reckon, and it is talking of winning four to five seats in the next Dáil. Is this wishful thinking or a realistic objective? Don Doyle quotes the good

---

12 *The Irish Times*, 28 May 1996.
13 www.ruc.police.uk.

results in 1997 of Martin Ferris in North Kerry (15.91 per cent of the votes, an increase of 13.54 per cent on the last election) or Sean Crowe in Dublin South West (with 8.9 per cent of the votes) in order to justify the aspirations of the party. But to consolidate its electoral base, Sinn Féin will have to encroach upon that of other parties. The task that lies ahead is difficult, given the fact that the vote transfer does not seem to benefit Sinn Féin much. While Sinn Féin voters tend to place in second position the Fianna Fáil candidate, in most cases the reverse does not happen. In the 1997 general election, Sinn Féin candidates received an average of merely 2 per cent of votes from Fianna Fáil transfers. Indeed, Fianna Fáil has sufficiently shown its attachment to republican principles to retain the votes of those who have always dreamed of a united Ireland but would not support armed struggle.

The left-wing vote might prove as difficult to conquer, given the limited impact of Sinn Féin's policies until now. Indeed, if the votes that are more likely to be transferred to Sinn Féin are those of the left-wing parties, the percentages are limited, ranging in 1997 from 5.48 per cent for the Workers' Party to 2.41 per cent for Democratic Left. Thus it seems that, for the time being, Sinn Féin candidates must, as Caoimhghín Ó Caoláin did, get a substantial number of votes the first time round and top the poll, since the transfer is not favourable to them.

The last general election took place before the second IRA ceasefire, and before the face-lift of the party had really had time to have an impact. Nevertheless, Sinn Féin's efforts seem to be paying off. At the local government elections in June 1999, the party significantly improved its first preference vote, almost doubling it to 3.5 per cent. Thus, Sinn Féin increased its representation in Dublin from one to four, and secured two seats in South Dublin, while it trebled its representation in Monaghan and won its first seat in Meath. Similarly, in the 1999 European elections, Sinn Féin doubled its vote, going from a national average of 3.21 per cent in 1994 to 6.34 per cent. Not surprisingly then, the party's Ard Comhairle is confident that 'the potential of Sinn Féin to grow and to provide to all the Irish people a real political alternative is enormous'.[14]

But in order to find its place within Irish political life, it will have to go beyond the border county vote and that of the underprivileged areas, and conquer the middle classes. Sinn Féin is multiplying initiatives in that direction, in an endeavour to penetrate social circles that had, until now, remained closed. Sinn Féin's spokespersons try to be heard at all levels of society. Mitchell McLaughlin thus addressed a SIPTU conference in Dublin. This, in itself, was not an entirely new fact: since the hunger strikes, Sinn Féin realised the importance of the union movement in its overall struggle. Gerry Kelly was invited to attend a conference by the Irish Film Centre. But more puzzling was the presence of Gerry Adams at a lunch of company directors organised by the Irish Institute of Directors in November 1998, in which he participated as guest speaker. His presence, which would have been unthinkable only one year before, undoubtedly reflects the new image that Sinn Féin is seeking to cultivate. It is also the result of important work from Sinn Féin's offices, which aim at ensuring that the party's voice is heard in the business community. The words of the Sinn Féin president did arouse some interest, undoubtedly mixed with scepticism: according to Sinn Féin's press office, the guests, usually around two hundred, numbered four hundred on that day, having come to hear Gerry Adams condemn the abuses of the Celtic Tiger and preach a policy of integration of the most disadvantaged.

Most Irish politicians are now taking Sinn Féin seriously as a political party. Abroad, Gerry Adams' name is probably better known than that of Bertie Ahern. During his visit to Mexico in November 1998, Adams was welcomed with great pomp and had a private meeting with the Minister for Foreign

---

14 Sinn Féin Ard Comhairle, *Political report to the Ard Fheis*, www.sinnfein.ie.

Affairs. Invited by Yasser Arafat to Palestine, Adams tours countries as a major international figure would. This perpetuates a long-standing tradition in republican strategies of internationalising the struggle by constituting a network of support and of lobby groups throughout the world. But what is new is that Sinn Féin's president has become the symbol of the transition from violence to negotiation. The welcome he got during his visit to the Basque Country in the autumn of 1998 was that of a statesman. Adams delivers a message of peace, and shares with his former comrades in struggle the lessons that Sinn Féin partly learned from the ANC. For the Basque nationalists of ETA, Adams is a guarantee of good faith, being the living proof that it is possible to lay down the guns and to go forward into negotiations without necessarily selling one's political soul.

Sinn Féin still has to prove to the Irish, north and south, that it is capable of managing the task it has set itself and that it is worthy of the trust that it is shown abroad. The serious crisis over decommissioning has put Sinn Féin's democratic commitment to the test. Whereas the unionist parties continue to mistrust their republican rivals, it seems that both the Irish and British governments are now prepared to accept that the party is acting in good faith on the issue.

Conclusion

Sinn Féin has travelled a long road since the 1994 IRA ceasefire. For decades it defined itself according to two different registers: those of nationalism and independence on the one hand and of socialism and liberation on the other. In so doing, it crystallised all the tensions and contradictions of this dual orientation. The difficulties of locating oneself, politically, at the meeting point of nationalism and socialism have been clearly identified by Rumpf and Hepburn.[15] Prior

---

15 E. Rumpf and A. C. Hepburn, *Nationalism and socialism in twentieth-century Ireland*, Liverpool: Liverpool University Press, 1977.

to the independence of the south, they claimed, the two aims of creating a national state and radically improving the living conditions of the 'lower classes' appeared to coincide: the national enemy was also the class enemy. In the south, this unity disintegrated after independence. The nationalist struggle took second place and was transformed into an aspiration, which was furthermore mediated by the state. The republican parties have played the social card and pursued populist causes in order to uphold their relevance as radical parties. In the north, the national issue continued to hold precedence in practical terms: radicalism manifested itself in the form of armed struggle.

The management of the tension between nationalism and socialism is by all accounts a difficult exercise. More so when a party which defines itself in terms of these two points of reference has to operate in situations in which they are combined differently. Retaining and even increasing its political relevance without collapsing into incoherence requires a highly skilled set of manoeuvres. The stakes are high, and there are no guarantees of success.

CHAPTER 5

Sport and Peace: An Uneasy Dialogue

ALAN BAIRNER

Since George Orwell first expressed the opinion that sport can best be described as 'war minus the shooting', and probably for much longer than that, the relationship between sport and conflict has been widely discussed. By its very nature sport tends to involve competition, which is relatively easy to situate on a spectrum that has war at its most dangerous extreme. Sports educators actually refer to certain activities as 'invasion' games, thereby evoking overt images of conflict and conquest. There is, of course, a substantial debate as to the precise role which sport can play in its guise as a form of warfare without weapons.

On the one hand, there are those who speak in terms of catharsis. Sport provides the vehicle through which people can express and act upon feelings of suspicion and downright hatred without causing too many casualties. Sport is a substitute for war. Indeed, according to the theory of the civilising process first propounded by Norbert Elias and Eric Dunning, sport performs a service by offering opportunities for the socially approved arousal of moderate excitement in public places, when social pressure has led people to exercise stricter control over their feelings and public displays of behaviour.[1] Studies of the 'Old Firm' rivalry in Scotland, for

---

1 N. Elias and E. Dunning, *Quest for excitement: Sport and leisure in the civilizing process*, Oxford: Blackwell, 1986.

example, have frequently focused on the idea that since sectarianism in other areas of Scottish life has virtually disappeared, football provides a convenient medium for the expression of residual hatred, thus channelling the problem away from mainstream social and political life. Alternatively, studies which are specifically concerned with the relationship between sport and the formation of particular identities have been more inclined to argue that sport reflects not only those feelings which can culminate in armed conflict but frequently exacerbates these feelings.[2] As a result, far from replacing war, sport can actually contribute to the creation of circumstances in which war becomes virtually inevitable. Thus, manifestations of sectarian animosity at games involving Celtic and Rangers have roots as well as implications that extend far beyond the confines of the stadia in which they are displayed. They not only reflect ongoing sectarian division in Scottish society but also help to ensure that it remains alive and influential. As a result, it can be argued that if the problem of sectarianism is to be tackled successfully in Scotland, the rivalry between Celtic and Rangers must be addressed directly. It cannot simply be assumed that the tension at their games will disappear over time as an inevitable by-product of the elimination of sectarian problems elsewhere in society.

Whilst debates of this type are relevant to the role of sport in all social formations, they are particularly pertinent when one is confronted with what have become generally recognised as deeply divided societies. The description itself is a curious one since all societies are deeply divided along at least one and probably along several fault lines. With regard to sport, all of these sources of division – gender, age, social class, sexual orientation and so on – are significant. The fault lines that are most closely identified with deeply divided societies, however, are associated specifically with ethnicity, race and

---

2 J. Sugden and A. Bairner (eds.), *Sport in divided societies*, Aachen: Meyer and Meyer, 1999.

national identity. Furthermore, these sources of division are extremely influential as regards sport, which not only reflects ethnic, racial and national divisions in such societies, but also serves to intensify these divisions. Sport contributes significantly to the construction and reproduction of certain identities and, by implication, to the maintenance of the gulf that exists between particular social groups. In this respect, the north of Ireland has been no different from a multitude of other deeply divided societies.

Gaelic games in Northern Ireland have contributed to the maintenance of a separate nationalist identity regardless of and, to some degree, in response to partition. British games such as rugby union have played a similar role in terms of the reproduction of unionist identity. In themselves, more universal games, most notably association football, have been more neutral as regards the formation of national identity. But because of the ways in which they have been organised, played and watched, they have facilitated inter-community competition which in turn has been of considerable importance in ensuring a continuing division between 'them' and 'us'. As with all matters relating to identity formation, however, the situation has always been more complex than these simple statements would suggest. As we shall see, the Gaelic Athletic Association (GAA) despite being organised on an all-Ireland basis, has increasingly looked like a rather different organisation depending upon which side of the border one has viewed its activities. Equally ironic is the fact that the all-Ireland organisation of some 'British' sports has created the situation in which northern unionists play for and support 'Irish' teams whatever their reservations may be about closer political or even economic links between the two parts of Ireland. Less surprisingly, soccer, with its world-wide capacity to heighten passions and from time to time to provoke violence, has persisted in providing a sporting arena for the acting out of ethno-sectarian divisions.

Those who study the relationship between sport and politics commonly ask what sport can do to help heal divisions. However, rather than focusing on that question, this chapter simply considers certain episodes in the world of Northern Irish sport which have taken place since the signing of the Good Friday Agreement. These can be shown to have political relevance particularly in terms of what they tell us about popular attitudes towards the peace process. Overall, like many other events in Northern Irish social and cultural life, some offer grounds for optimism and others indicate that the divisions which ensured the persistence of conflict for almost thirty years are still as deep as ever.

The three episodes chosen for this purpose are the debate about the GAA's Rule 21, which excludes British security forces personnel from membership; the heated discussion as to whether or not Donegal Celtic, a soccer team based in nationalist west Belfast, should have fulfilled a fixture in 1998 against the Royal Ulster Constabulary (RUC); and finally, the European Championship victory in early 1999 by Ulster's rugby union players and the accompanying claims that their stirring deeds had united the people of a traditionally divided society.

GAA Rule 21

There can be little doubt that the prevailing attitude within southern GAA circles supports moves towards the abandonment of Rule 21. In the north, however, whatever rank-and-file feelings may be, the official line taken by county boards has been for the ban to continue until such time as policing in Northern Ireland has been restructured. In the Irish Republic, the case for abandoning Rule 21 as part of the nationalist community's contribution towards the peace process may have seemed incontestable for all but a small republican minority. In the north, however, far more nationalists regarded the reasons for excluding members of the British security forces as being as strong as ever. They cited examples of harassment of GAA players and fans by members of the RUC and by British soldiers, particularly those belonging to the locally recruited Royal Irish Regiment. Constant reference was also made to those members of the

GAA who had been killed by the security forces and also by loyalist paramilitaries who are themselves widely regarded in republican circles as having acted in collusion with the security forces on a relatively regular basis. Furthermore, the occupation of GAA grounds by the security forces remains a burning issue, particularly in south Armagh where the highly successful Crossmaglen Rangers club has been seriously affected in this way. Despite all of this, however, there are many GAA members in the north who have felt for some time that the removal of Rule 21 would have been a timely gesture – a contribution to the peace process by a major element of Irish civil society. The fact that the retention of Rule 21 is by no means universally supported, even in the six counties, highlights divisions of a broader character within northern nationalism. The degree to which the issue can be largely understood in terms of a north–south divide, however, reflects deep-seated differences within Irish nationalism as a whole.

Donegal Celtic

Divisions within northern nationalism were also exemplified by the debate on whether or not the west Belfast soccer club, Donegal Celtic, should fulfil a fixture with the RUC during the 1998/9 season. A match involving the two clubs was scheduled to be played on 14 November 1998. Originally the mood in the local media, notably the nationalist *Andersonstown News*, was one of eager anticipation. Many people in the immediate area, however, expressed their anger that a soccer club based there should even contemplate having dealings with the footballers representing what they regarded as a discredited and wholly unacceptable police force. Feelings of this sort intensified as pressure on Donegal Celtic was increasingly applied by Relatives for Justice, a group representing families of people who had been killed by the RUC. Increasingly it was argued, even in the *Andersonstown News*, that playing the match would give offence to a substantial section of the local community. On 8 November, a majority of club members who attended a special meeting to discuss the issue voted in favour of playing the match. In the following days, however, rumours of visits being paid to the homes of Donegal Celtic officials and players grew and on 12 November the club's management, having been told by some players that they would be unable to play if the fixture were to go ahead, decided to withdraw from the competition.

Whilst many west Belfast nationalists supported this outcome, there were also large numbers who felt that Sinn Féin – which had come out openly against playing the match – had exceeded its remit in this instance and the rights of nationalist soccer fans in the area had been denied. At the purely sporting level, moreover, the whole episode highlighted the extent to which soccer (particularly in the shape of support for Glasgow Celtic) has maintained its status as the most popular sport in nationalist west Belfast, despite the overtures of the GAA. This may help to provide further insight into the republican movement's attitude towards the Donegal Celtic team. Certainly, amongst the purists within the GAA, there is a degree of disquiet at the fact that Gaelic clubs in the area are often used for the purposes of watching English premiership soccer.

What is undeniable is that, as a public relations exercise, Sinn Féin's strategy had been seriously flawed. Large numbers of west Belfast residents including many Sinn Féin voters (and soccer fans) expressed the view, usually in private, that on this occasion at least the party's representatives had wilfully ignored the wishes of many local people for narrow ideological reasons. Anecdotal evidence suggests that this unwanted outcome has been recognised by party leader, Gerry Adams. It was certainly imprudent at a delicate stage of the peace process for Sinn Féin to take for granted the votes of those who may have given the party a temporary mandate but are not yet wholly convinced by the party's commitment to peaceful politics. Denying such people a football match might seem like a relatively minor misdemeanour. But any evidence of arrogance or complacency is best avoided.

As regards the wider political context, the impact of the

Donegal Celtic saga has been to underline the fact that northern nationalism, particularly in the urban context, has never coalesced around a single, pure conception of Irishness. Although there are many who would regard both the Irish language and support for Gaelic games as being integral to their sense of identity, for others their Irishness is reproduced despite (and, in the case of following Celtic, by way of) activities which are deemed to be foreign in the eyes of the purists. Indeed, it should be noted that one of the main reasons why a junior club like Donegal Celtic attracts the degree of interest that it does is because west Belfast has had no senior soccer club since Belfast Celtic were forced to leave the league in 1949. The fact that this club had enjoyed enthusiastic support for over half a century is evidence that interest in the 'foreign' game in Belfast is in no way a new phenomenon occasioned by global cultural forces. Rather, support for soccer in Belfast (and, indeed, in Derry city) testifies to the game's close links to urbanisation and the growth of an industrial working class. Now, as in the past, the nationalist vision, as is revealed in this sporting example, is considerably less cohesive than some politicians might have us believe.

Rugby and Ulster nationalism

It has often been argued that the essence of Ulster unionism is essentially negative and that it relies predominantly on feelings of anti-Irishness. Less frequently expressed, however, is the view that northern nationalism has also tended to be fuelled by negative rather than positive sentiments. One such negative emotion surrounds the relationship of modern northern nationalists towards the very idea of Northern Ireland. In terms of sport, this is manifested most clearly in the lack of support in nationalist circles for the Northern Ireland soccer team despite the fact that it consistently contains players from both of the major communities.

Rugby union has traditionally assumed a rather different status in the eyes of northern nationalists. Organised, unlike

71

soccer, on an all-Ireland basis, and with a national team that represents the whole of Ireland, the game has contributed to the construction of Irish sporting nationalism. However, because of its British roots and the fact that in the north of Ireland it has tended to be played for the most part by middle-class unionists, the exploits of Ulster (and even Irish) rugby players have seldom caused excitement in northern nationalist, far less republican, circles.

Nevertheless, when Ulster played the French side Colomiers at Lansdowne Road on 31 January 1999 in the final of the European Cup, in attendance was not only Seamus Mallon, the leader of northern nationalists in the new assembly, but also his republican counterpart, Gerry Adams. One can only speculate on the reasons why these men were at a game which, certainly in the past, would have been of little interest to the people whom they represent. In public relations terms, their absence would have been noted. In sections of the British and Irish press, however, there were suggestions of genuine support amongst northern nationalists for the Ulster team. Undeniably such claims were greatly exaggerated, no doubt in the interests of creating a feel-good factor at a time when the peace process was facing severe difficulties. But Gaelic clubs did send messages of support to the Ulster rugby players and Catholics from the north did indeed travel to Lansdowne Road for the final. The presence of these Catholic fans, moreover, is indicative of the growing involvement of northern nationalists at all levels in a game that was once regarded as being alien to them. The extent of this involvement should not be exaggerated and the mass of Northern Ireland flags which were unfurled in Dublin on cup final day was clear evidence that rugby in the north is still a unionist game.

As the northern nationalist middle class has grown, however, inevitably the interest of Catholics in middle-class activities, including rugby, has also increased. Thus, whilst the endeavours of the Ulster rugby players may have had scant impact on sports fans in Ardoyne or Crossmaglen, there are signs that the cultural context within which the sport is

72

played in the north is changing. As this happens, however, sport will yet again reflect political and social cleavage. Even if substantial sections of the northern middle classes can set aside their sporting, and perhaps even their political, differences, working-class members of the rival traditions may find it less easy, or indeed desirable, to do so. When all is said and done, a triumph for the Irish rugby team still offers as little cause for celebration on the unionist Shankill as does a victory for the Ulster rugby players or the Northern Ireland soccer team on the nationalist Falls.

Sport and sectarianism

In the case of this particular conflict, therefore, sport reflects and contributes in certain ways to the context in which attempts to build and secure peace take place. At the same time, however, it continues to be intimately bound up with those divisions, both between and within communities, that make the ultimate prize so difficult to attain. It is evident from the rugby example that there is a constituency that now revels in its affluence and its cosmopolitanism, real or imagined. For such people, the peace process has to work inasmuch as it will create the kind of polite society in which old-fashioned differences can be set to one side in favour of greater pluralism and respect for diversity.

Both gaelic games and soccer, however, offer more evidence of the extent to which old animosities linger in certain areas and amongst certain groups of people. Some grains of comfort might be found in the fact that twice during the 1998/9 soccer season, Linfield Football Club, with its predominantly unionist support, were able for the first time since 1970 to fulfil fixtures at Solitude, the home ground of Cliftonville Football Club, based in north Belfast and mainly supported by nationalists. For almost thirty years, all games between the two clubs had been played at Linfield's ground, Windsor Park, or from time to time at neutral venues. It must be recognised, however, that the games only went ahead with severe restrictions having been imposed on the number of fans who were allowed to attend and against the backdrop of a massive security operation. Those seeking evidence of real political change will point to the fact that the games went ahead at all. The more pessimistic observers, on the other hand, noting the artificial context in which they took place, will remain unconvinced that the deep-seated sectarianism that lies at the heart of the conflict and remains a major obstacle to political progress, has been weakened in many areas of sport or indeed in most areas of the wider society.

The fact that the British security forces intend to withdraw from property owned by Crossmaglen Rangers GAA club has also been cited as evidence of progress, inasmuch as it might prompt the GAA to move more quickly towards rescinding Rule 21. Once again, however, a realistic assessment would suggest that this move will be interpreted by many northern Gaels as being simultaneously both a cosmetic exercise and the overdue righting of a manifest wrong. As a consequence, the removal of Rule 21 is almost certainly still dependent on policing reforms that are acceptable to a majority of northern nationalists.

In general, it can be seen that high profile sport in the north of Ireland is still more likely to strengthen the divisions that make peace so difficult to achieve than to help create the conditions in which a solution to the conflict can be found. Indeed, it would be asking too much to expect sport to succeed where politicians and church leaders have manifestly failed over many years. Sport in Northern Ireland does bring people together and can provide the basis for cross-community co-operation. It retains, however, an enormous capacity to reproduce sectarian identities. Indeed, unlike in more settled societies where, at worst, sport can be represented as a form of 'war without weapons', in the north of Ireland often it remains linked to the lingering threat of a return to 'war with weapons'.

THE TROUBLE WITH PROSPERITY

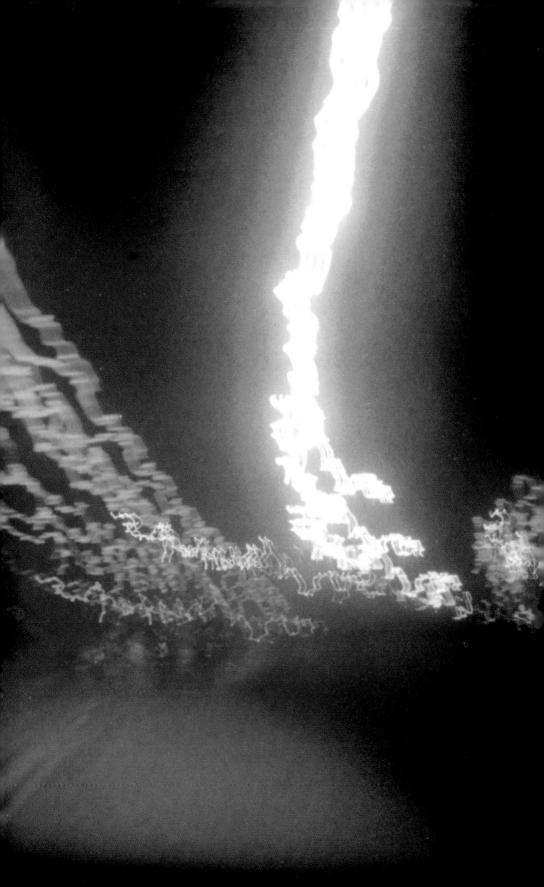

CHAPTER 6

Dublin's Car System

JAMES WICKHAM AND MARIA LOHAN

Suddenly, Dublin's traffic problem has become one of the defining features of the city. Yet, even as politicians and policy makers compete with each other to put forward solutions, there is also a widespread belief that the problem is a by-product of the country's economic progress, an almost natural event to be stoically borne.

By comparing Dublin to other cities in Europe and the world, this chapter shows that Dublin has become an extreme case of car dependency. It uses material from our EU-funded project on transport in four European cities: Athens, Bologna, Dublin and Helsinki.[1] In Dublin, as in Athens but unlike in Bologna and Helsinki, people's lifestyle has become dependent on the motor car. There is nothing inevitable about this: it is not the automatic result of economic growth or even of the city's low population density. The dependency is the result of socio-political choices.

In order to understand this, we use the argument from the sociology of technology which suggests that technological development proceeds along 'technological trajectories'. Once

---

1 Project SceneSusTech, Scenarios for a sustainable society: car transport systems and the sociology of embedded technologies, Contract: SOE1-CT97-1071.

these are entered, they are relatively difficult to change. This argument can be applied to the car and its infrastructure: the car system. Moving a city like Dublin towards more environmentally sustainable forms of mobility is difficult because the existing car system has become built into the city in a particular form: the car system is aligned with, and partly the result of, specific forms of public transport and specific forms of urban land planning. The car system is embedded in the physical fabric and the social interaction of each city. When you buy a car, and even more importantly when you use it, you are buying into a road system and even a particular sort of city.

The problem

Today in Dublin more people own cars than ever before. Walk around any middle-class Dublin housing estate and you will notice immediately that in many households the family car is being replaced by individuals' cars: driveways containing three or four cars are increasingly common. Our research project (SceneSusTech) has studied three areas of the city in detail: Jobstown (a suburban working-class area), Clonskeagh (a suburban middle-class area) and Docklands (a newly renovated inner-city area). In a survey of the three areas, just over half (56 per cent) of the households in Jobstown had a car, as compared to 89 per cent in Clonskeagh and only 39 per cent in the Docklands; in Clonskeagh 15 per cent of the households had three or more cars.

Cars are central to our current form of environmentally unsustainable development. High consumers of non-renewable energy resources, they also make a major contribution to global warming and the deterioration of the global environment. Road building uses vast amounts of non-renewable material, roads themselves eat up more and more space (up to 30 per cent of the land area in some US cities) and this by itself has environmental implications. At a local level, car emissions and car noise create local pollution. Equally, car accidents are now a major source of premature mortality and so an important public health issue.[2]

It is primarily for these reasons that car dependency is itself a problem. By car dependency we mean a situation in which people have become dependent on the car for many of their normal activities. Thus, in Ireland[3] in 1996, over 62 per cent of the population who travelled to work did so by car; in the Greater Dublin area this was 51 per cent.[4] In our study, about half of the people we interviewed in the suburban areas travelled to work or college by car (48 per cent in Jobstown, 53 per cent in Clonskeagh), although in Jobstown a significant proportion (15 per cent) had a lift in someone else's car. By contrast, in the inner-city Docklands, only 25 per cent used a car for this journey, largely because many are able to walk to work.

But far more is involved than simply travel to work. People use a car to deliver children to school, to do the shopping, to visit friends, to get medical attention. Thus, in Clonskeagh, over 53 per cent of our respondents travelled by car even to buy 'small amounts of food' and 69 per cent to visit a local doctor. There may be a choice between using the car and using an alternative form of transport, including walking. But the car itself offers greater choice, since it allows people to choose from a wider range of destinations: which shopping centre, which school, which friends, which doctor? At the same time, the choice is powerfully constrained by the very physical structures of roads and buildings. Many residential areas in Dublin are now built on the assumption that people have a car, so there are very few facilities in easy walking

---

2 For a summary of all these issues, see M. Lohan and J. Wickham, 'Literature review: car systems in European cities. Environment and social exclusion', Dublin: Trinity College Dublin Employment Research Centre, Report submitted to the European Commission, 1999. And, above all, J. Whitelegg, *Transport for a sustainable society. The case for Europe*, London and New York: Belhaven Press, 1993.

3 All figures refer to the Republic of Ireland.

4 Central Statistics Office, *Census 96, Volume 6: Travel to Work, School and College*, Dublin: Stationery Office, 1998.

distance. In Dublin, an increasing number of workplaces in the city's suburban office parks can only be reached by car. In many cities in the UK and above all in the US, facilities such as supermarkets and hospitals are increasingly centralised in a few suburban sites. The obvious example is the hypermarket, but the same may apply to hospitals and other public facilities.

Driving cars gives many people pleasure, a pleasure they would be very unwilling to give up. Yet to concentrate on the pleasure of owning and driving a car is to ignore the way in which many people's existing lifestyle has become impossible without the use of the car. For example, over two-thirds of our Dublin respondents who travelled to work or college by car felt that using public transport would be 'impractical'. Not surprisingly, therefore, most people who did not have a car would buy one 'if they could afford it', and this proportion is higher in the two suburban areas than in the Docklands. In the suburbs, the car is a necessity, unlike in the inner city. Reducing car dependency means changing lifestyles and/ or changing the physical construction of the city.

Car dependency can also create social exclusion. Even if everyone has a car, it is clear that the cost of owning and using a car is a relatively bigger burden on people with low incomes. Both Jobstown and Clonskeagh are built on the assumption that everyone, or at least every household, has a car; yet in Jobstown this is not the case. Journeys that are normal for the inhabitants of Clonskeagh are more likely to be complicated, time-consuming or even impossible in Jobstown. Thus, of all those who were in full-time jobs and who did not have a car, in Jobstown nearly half (46 per cent) felt that having a car would make getting to work easier, whereas this was the case for only 28 per cent in the Docklands.

Is car dependency inevitable?

Car dependency is normally seen as the inevitable result of an interaction between the market, technology and geography. As living standards rise, people choose to switch from public to private transport because it is more convenient, more comfortable and allows them greater choice. This growth of private transport in turn stimulates the growth of suburban housing and then subsequently suburbanised shopping, recreation and even employment. Consequently, high car use is the automatic consequence of low population density. Furthermore, this situation is inevitable; it is the automatic consequence of rising living standards. From such a per-spective, those who challenge the car are Don Quixotes, green fanatics doomed to defeat, because: 'there is no alternative, apart from lowering the living standards of ordinary people'.

One obvious way to evaluate this argument is to compare Dublin with other cities in the world that have comparable levels of income and similar population density. In order to do this Project SceneSusTech collected data on travel to work, population density and regional GNP in all our four case-study cities. We added this to similar data collected by an Australian research group on thirty-seven cities in Europe, eastern Asia, Australia and the US.[5] The evidence of Kenworthy et al. shows that automobile dependency is not inevitable. Car usage is not directly related to (city) income, but rather has a curvilinear relationship. At a certain level of income, car usage begins to level off as income continues to rise. They ascribe this to the development of effective mass transit systems (especially heavy rail) in affluent cities for relatively affluent groups; and a process of re-urbanisation as relatively affluent people move back into the inner-city.

Adding Athens, Bologna, Dublin and Helsinki to the data set strengthens this argument. Figure 1 plots the relationship between a city's wealth (the horizontal axis) and the extent

---

5 J. Kenworthy, F. Laube, P. Newman and P. Barter, *Indicators of transport efficiency in 37 global cities. A report for the World Bank*, Perth (Australia): Murdock University Sustainable Transport Research Group, 1997. Kenworthy et al. also collected data on Toronto. We have omitted Toronto from this analysis because it does not fall into any of the five groups into which the cities are divided (US, Australia, Europe, Developing Asian, Wealthy Asian).

to which people travel to work by private transport. The line linking the points on the chart shows how, as cities become richer, the extent to which people use private transport to travel to work rises, but then falls again. Secondly, the chart shows the clear difference between Europe and the US. In all the European cities in the sample, people are less likely to travel to work by private transport than in all the US cities. Thirdly, the chart shows that within Europe there is a very simple relationship between economic wealth and travel to work by private transport. The richer cities have lower levels of travel by private transport to work than the poorer cities. Of the four SceneSusTech cities, Dublin and Athens are the poorest, but they rely more on private transport than do Helsinki and Bologna.

Figure 1: *Wealth and journey to work (40 cities)*

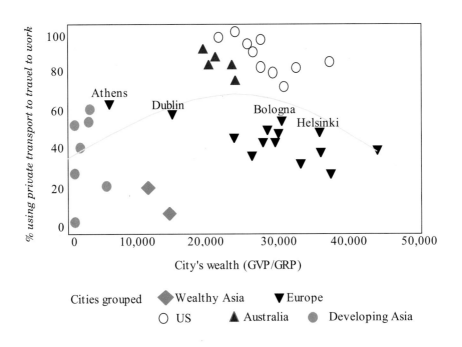

Source: SceneSusTech; Kenworthy et al.

The other argument used to explain Dublin's high reliance on private transport is its low population density. Outside the area between the two canals, Dublin is a suburban city. As Figure 2 shows, its population density is as low as that of many US and Australian cities. Despite this, Dubliners are still more likely to travel to work by public transport than American or Australian city-dwellers. Focusing only on the European cities makes the point even more clearly: there is no evidence for this type of relationship between population density and the way people travel to work. Indeed, of the four case-study cities, Helsinki has the lowest population density and the lowest use of private transport; Athens has the highest population density and the highest use of private transport.

Figure 2: *Population density and travel to work*

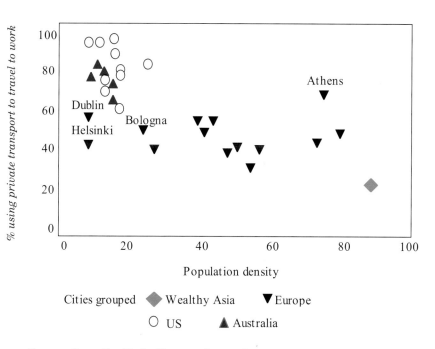

Source: SceneSusTech; Kenworthy et al.

This evidence shows that the usual explanations for Dublin's reliance on the private car are simply excuses. The socio-political choices that have led to Dublin's situation become clear when Dublin is compared with our other case-study cities.

A tale of four cities

The poorest of the four cities, Athens, has the highest level of car dependency in terms of travel to work. In fact, Athens seems a clear case of pathological levels of car dependency. It has the worst traffic jams, the worst pollution and the worst regulated parking of all our cities. At the same time there is effectively no viable alternative to the car for transport within the city, so that anyone who can possibly purchase a car does so. The car has driven out all other modes of transport, while deteriorating in efficiency itself. The dominance of the car contributes to a low quality of urban life and is itself both cause and effect of declining standards of urban citizenship. Athenians must use cars to move around their city, yet the only way to use the car is to break the law, even though this makes the situation worse for everyone. Although conditions in Dublin are not as extreme as in Athens, they are broadly similar: a high level of car dependency and a self-defeating pattern of car usage. There is some public transport but nothing that can be termed an effective public transport system. Dublin and Athens are becoming like the boom cities of South East Asia, epitomised by Bangkok: cities which are being swamped by the car, cities in which the traffic jam becomes a way of life.

Bologna and Helsinki, by contrast, have effective, even draconian, restrictions on the use of the private car in their central areas. In each city, these historic centres provide their citizens with pleasant and attractive urban environments that are focal points for the city as a whole. In both Bologna and Helsinki, the city centre is an attractive destination in its own right, rather than merely the location of isolated historic buildings and tourist destinations. The *centro storico* of Bologna in particular is an exemplar of one aspect of the European urban ideal. In both cities, mobility in the central area is almost exclusively by public transport: by high quality buses in Bologna, by buses and trams in Helsinki. Outside of the centres of all four cities, transport depends more heavily on the car. However, differences remain. Helsinki in particular combines quite extensive public transport in the form of metro, suburban rail and bus with a well-functioning road network, thus ensuring that its citizens are able to move around the city area relatively easily.

We begin to understand how these differences have occurred by looking at the historical relationship between the city and the nation. Both Dublin and Helsinki are capital cities of small European countries; neither of which existed as sovereign states in 1900. In both countries, a nationalist movement won independence at the end of World War I. Both nationalist movements were cultural as well as political, but in the Finnish case the new national state was strongly identified with the city of Helsinki. The historical buildings of the nineteenth century were identified as part of what we would now call national heritage. Furthermore, a new national style of monumental architecture was central to Finnish nationalism in the early twentieth century, and the key buildings of this style were built in Helsinki. Accordingly, any planning decision in Kantakaupunki, the central core of the city, is a matter of major public concern.

By contrast, although Dublin was the centre of much political activity in the struggle for independence, the actual physical structure of the city was defined as an alien English (Protestant) imposition on the pure body of Catholic Ireland. The period of the rise of Irish nationalism in the nineteenth century was also a time when Dublin was in relative decline. While in the nineteenth century the ruling elites of many European cities had their own projects of municipal glorification, the physical structure of Dublin deteriorated under a political leadership that had much more limited civic objectives. Such history helps to explain how politicians, and citizens, can have very different priorities in different cities.

Another historical inheritance is the role of previous public transport systems, what we might call 'legacy systems'. The question here is the extent to which physical structures from a previous epoch continue into the present. In 1900, Dublin probably had the best public transport system of our four cities. It had several suburban railway lines and a newly electrified tram system covering the inner-city area. While much of this was built within an existing city, Helsinki had grown on the basis of its tram and above all its railway lines. The inter-war period established the conditions for Dublin's subsequent transport decline, and Helsinki's subsequent success. During the 1920s, the private company that owned the Dublin tram system replaced trams with buses and was able to ensure government legislation to give it a monopoly status. By contrast, the Helsinki tram system continued to be expanded in the inter-war period, even though buses were also being used. In Dublin, the profit-maximising strategy of the private owners ensured the destruction of the tram system, whereas in Helsinki municipal ownership conserved public transport. When the revival of public transport began in Helsinki in the 1970s, there were considerable resources for development, while by this time Dublin was left with merely some remnants of its old suburban rail system.

One factor that determines what cities do with these cultural resources is the power of local government to make effective land use plans and to link these to transport plans. In Athens, legislation from 1983 and 1985 imposes on local authorities the obligation to draw up urban plans, but, in practice, growth in Athens has been unregulated and unplanned. The key feature of Athens' local government therefore is its lack of capacity or ability to act. There is only a very limited relationship between legislation and what actually happens on the ground and, furthermore, to the extent that any policy does get implemented, this depends on central government for both conception and execution.

Urban planning in Dublin shows many similar features. While formally there now is a Dublin regional authority, it has no real powers, and planning functions within the metropolitan area depend on four different local authorities. In this framework, planning is continually adjusted by various political deals, so that in practice planning is replaced by developer-led development.[6] Just as it was largely the private decision of the transport owners that destroyed the previous tramway system, so the location of housing, shopping and other facilities (especially in the suburbs) is essentially the result of the decisions of property developers. Whereas in Athens plans are simply ignored, in Dublin they are subverted. In both cases, however, the physical structure of the city has been determined by individual private interests. Equally, although Dublin's formal planning procedures allow for extensive participation, the reality is public apathy. The city has simply grown in its present highly suburbanised form without any generalised political discussion.

Our other two cities provide a clear contrast. In Helsinki, although there was some competition between the component municipalities in the 1960s, overall planning authority has been successfully exerted since the 1970s. A metropolitan area council provides a framework for greater Helsinki, but real power remains at the municipal level. However, unlike in Dublin, Helsinki's city council has enough financial independence and legislative authority to provide local government with high capacity. Its planning powers have ensured that suburban development, whether of housing, employment or retail trade, is concentrated at public transport nodes. Its financial autonomy has enabled it to develop an integrated public transport system. In particular, the decision to build a metro system was taken at city, not at national, level. Similarly, in Italy, regional and city governments have both power and financial autonomy. This provides the framework within which Bologna's city council has been able to plan the transport system as part of a general strategy for reconciling the need for mobility with the need to preserve the city's historic core.

---

6   Note that it is this structure that generates the possibility of bribery.

Conclusion

Overall, Athens and Dublin clearly emerge as the two 'worst practice' cities. To what extent do very recent developments promise a change for the better?

In Dublin, in early 1999, policy proposals were announced that aim at increasing housing density, increasing public transport provision and concentrating development at pubic transport nodes.[7] Yet these are only proposals. On the ground, the reality is that EU structural funds continue to be used to increase car dependency through major infrastructural investment in roads (especially the M50 ring road).

In both cities, there are now large-scale rail projects (the Athens metro, the Dublin light rail system). These do indicate a clear break with previous policy in that they are substantial investments in public transport. Quite apart from the fact that it is not yet certain that the Dublin project will be built, both projects continue and even exacerbate the political tradition that major decisions are made by national government. If anything, they reduce the capacity of the metropolitan decision-making system. A necessary (but certainly not sufficient) precondition for reducing Dublin's car dependency is the city gaining some political autonomy and control over itself.

---

7 See the two reports on housing policy (Peter Bacon and Associates, 1998 and 1999) and the strategic guidelines for the Dublin region (Brady Shipman and Martin Consultants, 1999).

Echelon Parking

Do Not Cross the Line

Forward In - Back Out

Pedestrian Crossing

Look Both Ways

TAXI

GREEN Car Park

YELLOW Car Park

EXIT

Vehicles are parked at owners risk only. The owners of the centre will not be responsible for damage to vehicles or for property stolen from vehicles parked here

CHAPTER 7

Mall City*

MARY P. CORCORAN

Since the 1960s, Dublin has been turning itself inside out. The boundaries of the city have continued to expand in a seemingly relentless process of ex-urbanisation, whereby housing, factories and, most recently, shopping and entertainment facilities are increasingly located on the city's outskirts. In the case of Dublin, ex-urbanisation has historically been supported by the institutions of the state. In the 1960s, University College Dublin, Radio Telefís Éireann and numerous city-based schools and hospitals relocated to the suburbs. In the 1970s, most private and state investment, not only in housing but also in retail, was channelled into suburban areas.[1] Despite the regeneration of urban centres that was set in motion by the introduction of urban renewal schemes in 1985, the exodus is still under-way. Most recently, a number of major city centre hospitals have been consolidated into a suburban 'super' hospital at Tallaght. In a controversial move, the Central Sorting Office of An Post relocated from Sheriff Street to an industrial

---

*   The photographs in this chapter have been reproduced courtesy of The Square Management Company; Liffey Valley Shopping Centre; and Green Property Management Ltd, The Blanchardstown Centre.
1   K. McKeown, 'Urbanism in the Republic of Ireland: A conflict approach', in P. Clancy et al. (eds.), *Ireland: A sociological profile*, Dublin: Institute of Public Administration, 1986, pp. 326–43.

estate in west Dublin. In a classic case of urban displacement, the old sorting office building has been revamped into an architecturally acclaimed private office development which now forms part of the International Financial Services Centre. The ex-urbanised city now climbs to the foothills of the Dublin mountains and sweeps down to the seaside towns of north Wicklow, also extending northward and westward beyond the county boundaries. On the perimeter of the city, industrial estates, business parks and, most recently, shopping malls have sprung up, all of which are linked through a series of ring roads and motorways.

The argument that I will pose in this chapter is twofold. Firstly, I will suggest that the spatial form a city takes is shaped fundamentally by endogenous political economic forces, with the state playing a crucial role in this process of urban transformation. Secondly, the recent development of shopping mall culture in Dublin reveals a tension between the concepts of public and private. Although ostensibly a public good, accessible to all, in reality the new shopping malls are predicated on a consumer class with spending power and access to private vehicles. The concept of public space for the use of a civic community is somewhat usurped by shopping mall management who attempt to foster a community or town centre function on private property that is regulated by private policing.

The state and shopping mall production

A recent feature of the ex-urbanisation process has been the proliferation of a particular kind of cathedral of consumption: the out-of-town shopping mall. The first of these to be completed was the Tallaght Town Centre (the Square), located on the N11 roadway, which opened in 1990. The success of the Square resulted in its adoption as a prototype for a series of shopping malls on the perimeter of the city, each located close to a major thoroughfare: the Omni Centre near the M1 motorway, the Blanchardstown Centre located near the N3, and the Liffey Valley Centre on the N4 route to the west.

New shopping malls are in the pipeline at Clondalkin, Swords and Malahide.

The Square was developed by a consortium made up of the Irish-owned Monarch Properties and the British-based Guardian Royal Exchange. To ensure that the development went ahead, the Square was granted designated area status under the urban renewal scheme originally introduced by the state in 1985. Designated status was granted despite the fact that, as a green field site, the proposed development did not conform to the definition of urban renewal. It was widely recognised, however, that Tallaght, as a major population centre on the periphery of the city, was in need of infrastructural development. In co-operation with developers, the state sought through its fiscal policies to create the conditions conducive to such development. All the original tenants taking up leases in Tallaght Town Centre were given a tax allowance of 100 per cent of the construction costs of their shop units against trading income. There was also double rent allowance against trading income for a period of ten years and a full remission of rates for the same period. In addition, there was an initial tax allowance of 50 per cent in the case of a lessor or investor taking up a stake in the complex. For the major multiples in particular, the tax advantages were highly attractive. The commercial success of the Square can be gleaned from the fact that average rents (which qualify for double tax relief) are one-third to twice as high as rents in the nearest shopping centre.[2] Through its promotion of the Tallaght Town Centre, the state provided the impetus for out-of-town shopping, instigating a rush of developer-led development as British–Irish consortia scrambled to acquire sites along the lucrative M50 route. The key players are now British-owned multiples, whose profit margins are considerably higher than those of their Irish counterparts.

2   *Study on the urban renewal schemes*, prepared by KPMG in association with Murray O'Laoire Associates and the Northern Ireland Economic Research Centre, Dublin: Department of the Environment, 1996, p. 59.

Although designated status was not accorded to the out-of-town shopping centres that followed on the heels of the Tallaght Town Centre, the state had indeed played an indirect role in their advancement. Out-of-town shopping could not have thrived without massive infrastructural investment in the motorway and adjacent roadways network. Shopping malls, given their spatial organisation and location, are primarily built for a particularly type of consumer, the consumer who has access to a private car. Hundreds of thousands of shoppers drive to these shopping malls every week. The success of the malls is indicative of the rise in consumer spending in the economy as a whole. More pertinently, it indicates that the relationship between citizens and urban public space is changing, as people vote with their wallets and their cars. The notion of accessibility via private transport has been a key strategy in the marketing of Dublin's major shopping malls. When the Square opened in Tallaght in the early 1990s, its (then) unrivalled accessibility was flagged by the developers: a shopping centre that could be reached in thirty minutes or less drive time by one million potential customers. More recently, the developers of the Liffey Valley Centre spent several million pounds realigning the nearby primary roadway in order to maximise customer access to the shopping mall. The concept of motorway accessibility became an integral part of the centre's launch campaign: 'What do you get when you cross the M50 with the N4?', read the advertisements and billboards. Answer: 'The Liffey Valley Experience'. The developers estimated that the centre would have 1.45 million potential customers who would drive from as far afield as Mullingar, County Westmeath some fifty or so miles away.[3]

One immediate effect of the shopping malls is to increase traffic volume. The unlimited parking facility (each shopping mall is surrounded by acres of free parking spaces) is marketed as a key incentive to the car-using public. The

---

3   B. Harrison, 'Temple of Boom', *The Irish Times*, 10 October 1998.

Car parking, Liffey Valley Centre

shopping mall phenomenon is, therefore, inextricably bound up with the growth in our car culture. But if cars are crucial to gain access to the new means of consumption, it follows that those without cars will be to some degree socially excluded. More than 40 per cent of urban households in Ireland have no car, a figure that has hardly altered since the beginning of the 1990s.[4]

In addition to the direct and indirect inducements outlined above, changes at the level of the local state also contributed to the out-of-town shopping mall phenomenon. The division of Dublin city and county into four separate local authorities in the mid-1990s created the conditions for unregulated development. As analysts have pointed out, since the abolition of household rates there is a commercial imperative on each local authority to maximise its commercial rates income. For that reason, local authorities are generally predisposed toward prospective developers.[5]

---

4 F. Convery, *Large-scale out-of-town shopping developments in Ireland. Issues and choices*, Dublin: Musgrave Group, 1999, p. 11.
5 J. Bruder, 'Getting the balance right', *The Irish Times*, 18 March 1998.

The Irish state's transformative role has facilitated not only the creation of new productive capacities, but also the means through which new consumption capacities can be deployed. At national level, direct fiscal subsidies and indirect infrastructural investment acted as catalysts for out-of-town shopping mall development. At local level, networks were fostered between state officials, politicians and commercial developers. It is clear then that Irish policy-makers have followed what Evans describes as a developmental model in relation to the new means of consumption. State agencies have been 'embedded in a concrete set of social ties that binds the state to society and provides institutionalised channels for the continual negotiation and re-negotiation of goals and policies'.[6] Such a strategy allows the state sufficient autonomy to transcend where necessary the individual interests of its private counterparts in order to resolve collective problems.

Once initiated, shopping mall development in Dublin spiralled out of control so that by the end of the 1990s analysts were expressing fears that the area was becoming 'over-shopped'. In 1998, the state decided to restrict the size of new supermarkets pending a review of the implications of large-scale shopping centres, demonstrating how a flexible developmental strategy works in practice. This would appear to be a belated recognition that the shopping mall boom inevitably comes at a cost. The state bolstered Dublin's retail boom, but in the process seems to have accentuated social inequalities not only between consumers, but also between regions and locales. Shopping malls draw consumers away from local shopping centres, because they centralise the shopping function. At the same time, they contribute to the decentralisation of the city and make the shopping function more and more dependent on car accessibility. The more the shopping mall reshapes the notion of what constitutes

6   P. Evans, *Embedded autonomy*, Princeton: Princeton University, 1995, p. 12.

shopping in the social imaginary the less possible it will be to return to, much less imagine, alternative means of consumption.

The social construction of malls

Dublin's shopping malls have imposed themselves in a spectacular way on the outer city landscape. Driving southwestward on the N11 there is little to distract the eye. The road takes you through large tracts of social housing, each estate virtually indistinguishable from the next. And then, a glass pyramid is suddenly visible, the apex of the Square boldly bisecting the sky. An icon drawn from the ancient past, the pyramid dominates the landscape for miles around. As a symbol, it signifies the regeneration of Tallaght, and it also functions as an important landmark. It is instantly recognisable and inescapable. The Liffey Valley Centre, sited on formerly agricultural land along the N4 in west Dublin, draws its inspiration from the future; its cluster of dome-topped buildings looks remarkably like a space station. In their promotional literature, Dublin's shopping malls make much of their 'bigness', in terms of their actual size, the number of outlets they contain, the number of parking places available to customers and the volume of throughput or 'footfall' figures. Bigness becomes an important element of public place making, to the extent that the Tallaght Town Centre asserts that there is 'nowhere bigger, nowhere better'.

These shopping malls are brand-new places that have been materially and symbolically constructed out of empty space. They represent the commodification of landscape both in terms of its external and internal configurations. The effect of their formulaic construction, however, is that there is 'a weakening of the identity of places to the point where they not only look alike but feel alike and offer the same bland possibilities of experience'.[7] The malls are approached

---

7   E. Relph, *Place and placelessness*, London: Pion, 1976, p. 89.

through a network of anonymous roadways and are surrounded by acres of no-man's-land car parking space. Their internal landscapes carry through the idea of spectacle, albeit in a commodified form. Nature is either faithfully reproduced (natural forms of vegetation and real trees) or re-invented in easier to manage forms (faux trees of unusual colour). Water cascades down the enclosed waterfall at the Square in Tallaght, and shimmers in the central fountain at the Blanchardstown Centre. A sense of spectacle (something to look at) is created, at the same time as the consumer is invited to make a connection with nature, thus fulfilling a human need.[8]

Indoor tree, the
Blanchardstown Centre

8   G. Ritzer, *Enchanting a disenchanted world*, Thousand Oaks, CA: Pine Forge Press, 1999, p. 9.

*Water detail,
the Square, Tallaght*

While the marble, steel and plastic are clearly functional, the adornments – in the form of glass elevators, moving water, sculptures, vegetation and trees – are there to enchant. In this sense, the shopping mall as spectacle exists as a space of representation: a space in which the social imaginary is opened to new visions.

Private space masquerading as public space

The shopping mall is a place that is protected, a space that is controlled, a space that constitutes a separate world. But it works hard at giving the impression that it is not controlled, and that it is merely a continuation of the customer's existing social world. The shopping mall offers the consumption equivalent of life in a gated community. 'By creating a secure environment in which buying is the whole point, the mall psychologically links the idea of safety with the idea of shopping. But it must do more than that: it must take practical steps to ensure the mall's actual security.'[9] To preserve the illusion of an open public space, however, measures taken must be low-key and not immediately evident to the customer.

Thus, the shopping mall must sustain its particular sense of social reality through a process of mystification. The customer must be put at ease, but must not be made aware of the effort that goes into creating this sense of ease. Inside the shopping mall is a tightly regulated world constituted by privately owned and controlled consumption space. There are clearly marked entrances and exits, helpfully colour-coded in the case of Blanchardstown and the Liffey Valley Centre. Visitors cannot get lost, nor lose themselves, as all paths taken ultimately lead somewhere.

Concealed entrances within the shopping malls lead to backstage areas housing an entire managerial system, with offices, security systems, public relations agents and so on. The shopping mall is a commercial operation and investments must be protected. Hence, management engage in a high level of surveillance. Each shopping mall has its own security team who constantly patrol the public aisles in order to safeguard the secure, trouble-free ambience. They are supplemented in this task by closed-circuit television systems. Security systems are also in operation to keep shoppers' cars under surveillance while they are parked. Considerable effort is invested then in the staging of an authentic shopping experience, all orchestrated from the management centre within the heart of the complex.

This contrasts dramatically with the unstaged authenticity of the city centre streets. The latter tend to be noisy, dusty, crowded, and filled with different kinds of people. (Although

---

9   W. Kowinski, *The malling of America*, New York: William Morton, 1985, p. 360.

it must be acknowledged that recent trends, such as the introduction of closed-circuit television on city streets and attempts to thwart young people from congregating in public areas, indicate the diffusion of surveillance strategies beyond the privately owned malls.) Malls are much more controlled environments, which render the shopping experience a highly predictable one. There are no scam artists, no panhandlers, no buskers, nobody sleeping in doorways, no dogs' dirt on the walkways. Men in suits check out the clientele and chuck out those who do not conform. The feeling of safety one experiences in a shopping mall is a direct outcome of the security measures taken, although customers are generally not privy to the policing function. The mall appears to be public space open to all, but in fact 'malls are private property, [where] one is subject to the rules of the mall builder and operator in addition to the civil laws applying to public places'.[10] The socially stigmatised, including those with limited means of consumption, are conspicuous by their absence from the shopping mall. Given the high levels of surveillance and control, little opportunity is provided to express resistance to exclusionary policies.

At the behest of management, however, the private space can be turned over to the community to be used as public space. Through all kinds of organised events from graduation ceremonies to fashion shows to choir performances at Christmas time, the shopping mall offers its customers the opportunity to participate in community activities as defined by the mall management. Such staged events are designed to generate feelings of intimacy and experiences that can be talked about as participation.[11] Staged events also provide an excellent public relations opportunity for the management, as well as creating an attraction which can help to fill the

10 J. Jacobs, *The Mall: An attempted escape from everyday life,* Prospect Height, IL: Waveland Press, 1984.
11 D. MacCannell, 'Staged authenticity: Arrangements of social space in tourist settings', *American Journal of Sociology,* vol. 79, no. 3, 1973, p. 601.

Restaurant, the Square, Tallaght

mall, especially on prime shopping days. For example, one shopping mall staged an Irish dancing exhibition on St Patrick's Day 1999, which created a community focal point for the centre as 'somewhere to go' on a day when, traditionally, city centre stores shut.

Similarly, the shopping malls operate a policy of business as usual on Sundays. One chaplain who services a shopping mall oratory remarked that a trip to the shopping mall on a Sunday afternoon has replaced the traditional family visit to the graveyard. The family that shops together, stays together! Furthermore, by creating space within the complexes for local services, such as post offices, oratories, solicitors' centres, libraries and one-stop shops, the shopping mall developers are further appropriating Main Street as the focal point of community and relocating it within the cathedrals of consumption.

Conclusion

'Malls, as interventions in the fabric of urban public space, are fragments of broader changes in the system of spatiality and concrete spatial practices at global, national and local scales.'[12] The spatial differentiation currently underway in the greater Dublin area is resulting in increased cosmopolitanism, diversification and ethnicisation at the centre, and increased homogenisation of the consumption function through shopping mall development on the periphery. The relationship between Dublin's citizenry and urban space is altered in light of the development of these new means of consumption. Shopping malls are creating new forms of stratification in the economy and in the realm of consumption. Citizenship is being redefined as the capacity to participate in the new means of consumption.

A number of processes are at work. Firstly, the centralisation of shopping in the malls on the perimeter of the city impacts on local shopping centres in Dublin and the surrounding counties. It can be argued that the shopping malls are undermining the economic wellbeing of both (smaller) urban and rural communities. Secondly, the rise of the shopping mall implies the decentralisation of shopping and related services from the city centre into places where access is predicated on ownership of a car. Thirdly, malls engage in a process of mystification that blurs the distinction between public and private space. Private space is symbolically represented as open public space through the clever orchestrations of management, security staff and cleaners whose work takes place primarily backstage. Aisles gleam, civility reigns, safety is guaranteed. Customers are encouraged to identify positively with the mall through the management's commitment to staging certain types of community events and providing space for community services. Thus, shopping malls require customers to renegotiate their understanding of, and relationship to, consumption and community.

---

12 R. Shields, 'Social spatialisation and the built environment: the West Edmonton Mall', *Environment and Planning D: Society and Space*, vol. 7, 1989, p. 147.

IF YOU ARE COMING WITH GOOD WILL...

YOU ARE ALWAYS WELCOME T

Sarajevo

CHAPTER 8

Strangers in our Midst

MICHEL PEILLON

In the late summer of 1998, a Tullamore doctor announced that he was offering a reward of £10,000 to trace the origin of rumours circulating about him in this small town in the Midlands. The rumours related to the unexplained disappearance of a young mother from the town. Not only was the doctor alleged to be involved in this disappearance, but all kinds of sinister crimes and practices were mentioned. The doctor's announcement hit the headlines and he was interviewed on the main television news programmes. When the image of this mild-mannered individual with his wife and children appeared on screen, the real issue in this episode became obvious. As an Eastern, Muslim family in the middle of a culturally homogeneous small town, they had been targeted by a campaign of nasty rumours. Whatever the motives or interests of those who started these rumours, a sufficient number of people were willing to believe or half-believe this story, to carry it around and spread it, to uphold its plausibility within the collectivity. For a brief time, one glimpsed the uglier side of Irish provincial life.

Only a little more than two thousand non-nationals resided in Ireland in 1939.[1] Now the figure has risen, according to

---

1 D. Keogh, *Jews in twentieth century Ireland. Refugees, anti-Semitism and the Holocaust*, Cork: Cork University Press, 1998.

very rough estimates, to close to 4 per cent of the population in the Republic of Ireland. English, Welsh and Scots staying in Ireland are numbered with difficulty, as a long-standing agreement between the UK and Ireland grants to nationals of both countries reciprocal rights of travel, residence and work. The same now applies to residents of other EU countries; a figure of 100,000 EU nationals living in Ireland has been put forward. Around 25,000 non-EU nationals are said to reside in Ireland. The first Chinese arrived in the 1960s and they now form a community of 11,000 people; most of whom work in Chinese restaurants. The door was opened in 1979 to a limited number of refugees from Vietnam. Around 600 Boat People, as they were then called, have settled here. The recent dismantling of Yugoslavia and the ensuing civil war led to another wave of refugees in 1992; more than 800 Bosnians now live in Ireland. An increasing number of Muslims reside here; officially recorded at 3,875 in the 1991 Census, their numbers have rapidly increased to 6,000. Five hundred Indian nationals are also registered in Ireland.

Concern has emerged more recently about the increasing number of people seeking political asylum in Ireland. Practically nobody looked for refuge in Ireland a few years ago. In 1992, only thirty-nine individuals applied for refugee status. In 1995, the figure remained low at 424 applications. In 1997, the number of applications rose to 4,626 and then to 7,724 in 1999. Applicants for refugee status typically come from countries such as Congo, Nigeria, Algeria and Somalia, and a high proportion of these applications have been rejected. More recently, refugees from eastern Europe have appeared on the Irish scene, most of them Romanian gypsies attracted to Ireland by rumours of prosperity and generosity.

A negative attitude has developed of late in Ireland towards 'foreigners', or rather towards some categories of foreigners. They are now perceived as a threat and they trigger mechanisms of social closure. This chapter is concerned with answering the questions of why and how this happens. Hostility towards foreigners, or even towards cultural minorities, is conventionally explained in terms of intolerance towards those with a different culture. A rather different view is put across in this chapter. It is argued that those groups, strangers in our midst, attract hostility to the extent that they cannot balance their participation in the host society: that, for reasons which are often outside their control, what they are perceived to draw from the group is not matched by what they give to it.

A question of culture?

Prejudice is usually directed at those people who do not adopt our mores or share our values. They live according to ways which deviate from those of the host country; they retain in their appearance and demeanour something of the place they came from. They are judged in the light of their distance from the cultural standards of the host country and inevitably fare badly in the exercise. Their existence is acknowledged only through their difference. For this reason, these cultural minorities attract like a magnet practices of rejection and hostility. But a culturalist account of prejudice reaches deeper than pointing out cultural differences. It would contend, for instance, that the increased hostility towards foreigners in Ireland is explained in terms of a growing threat to an Irish identity: a sense that tradition is dissolving and lifestyle eroding. 'Group boundaries may thus be generated by uncertainty', contends Richard Jenkins.[2] Continuous change, by itself, would trigger a process of closure, as a response to the disappearance of stable cultural points of reference.

A link is actually observed between the level of cultural differences and the degree of social distance.[3] Micheál MacGréil, in his study of prejudice in Ireland, has measured

---

2 R. Jenkins, *Social identity*, London: Routledge, 1996, p. 214.
3 Social distance refers, in MacGréil's study, to a measure of how close people are prepared to admit members of various categories: as family members, friends, neighbours, colleagues, citizens, visitors to the country.

the attitudes of Irish people towards a wide range of social, ethnic and national categories.[4] No great social distance is recorded for English, North Americans, Scots and Welsh; their rating is explained by the author in terms of ethnic propinquity. This category includes those nationalities which, culturally very close, have been the traditional destination of Irish emigration. In any case, the otherness of this category of people is hardly registered; accent sets them apart, but they still share a language and many cultural traits. Nationals from other western European countries elicit a little more social distance. But Ireland has moved quite close to western Europe in political, economic and even cultural terms.

Irish people do not feel particularly close to a range of nationalities or ethnicities: less than half, for instance, would accept Jews, Greeks, Russians or Africans into their families. Chinese, Blacks, Indians, Israelis, Nigerians, Black Americans, Pakistanis, Muslims, Arabs and Travellers, all score high on social distance. Most contemporary nationalities and ethnicities outside the English-speaking world and western Europe are included in this category. This evidence needs to be interpreted with some caution, and it does not necessarily support an explanation exclusively in terms of cultural differences. Other criteria seem to be involved. For instance, although sharing in many ways a basic American culture, a far greater level of intolerance is directed at 'Black Americans' than at Americans in general.

A first point can be used to unsettle the culturalist account. The very idea of identity appears suspect nowadays. The assertion of an Irish identity would imply that the inhabitants of Ireland share attitudes, values, beliefs and cultural orientations. It points to a tradition, a collective experience which has moulded the very being of the people. The discourse of identity ends up relying on generalisations and it makes

---

4   M. MacGréil, *Prejudice in Ireland revisited*, Maynooth: St Patrick's College, 1996.

heavy use of stereotypes. Identity postulates a cultural unity, through which the diversity of Ireland is reduced to a common framework. 'Belief in a single identity, spirit or soul; belief in a unified unconscious for the group or the race; belief in the dominance of a complex of beliefs or mores or institutions; all these beliefs are vague, uncritical, misleading and even politically dangerous.'[5] When identity is given a fixed content, then the upholding of identity requires that group boundaries are policed: to reject everything which may dilute its tradition; to react against what risks weakening it; to contain the threat of a contagious difference. But it is not clear which features of Irishness are threatened by the presence in Ireland of people with different ways.

The second argument which militates against the culturalist account of intolerance stresses the fact that rejection and prejudice is differentiated. Many people have come to reside in Ireland and they have made their homes here. They have been, by and large, tolerated, although to very different degrees. Only specific groups of foreigners attract hostility. Coexistence has remained quite harmonious with the Chinese minority in Ireland, with the Bosnian refugees or even, perhaps to a lesser extent, with the Muslim community. Not all 'foreigners' are placed in the same category or generate the same level of rejection. The cultural account would still hold if it could be shown that the level of prejudice and intolerance is associated with the relative distance between indigenous and foreign cultures. Those who are the furthest away in cultural terms would experience most hostility and rejection. Such a demonstration is not easily made.

The third and possibly the strongest argument against the culturalist interpretation concerns the fact that the level of cultural identification is not related to the level of

5   D. Moran, 'Wandering from the path: Naviguio in the philosophy of John Scottus Eriugena', in M. P. Hederman and R. Kearney (eds.), *The Crane Bag book of Irish studies*, Dublin: Blackwater Press, 1982.

intolerance. Micheál MacGréil, in his above-mentioned study of prejudice and tolerance in Ireland, has measured what he calls the level of Irish identification (which refers to the extent to which people define themselves as Irish). He has also provided measures of 'social distance' and 'racialism' as indications of prejudice and intolerance. The culturalist argument postulates a link between identification with Irish culture and negative attitudes towards those who deviate from Irish cultural standards. In fact, a reverse relationship emerges. Those social categories which express the strongest sense of Irish identification also manifest greater tolerance towards foreigners and uphold the least racialist attitudes: those living in large urban areas, those with a more formal education, those with a high occupational status and the higher social classes.

The cohabitation of different cultures produces its daily tensions, and foreign practices often deeply offend the cultural standards of a society. But the root of rejection is to be found elsewhere and another type of explanation is required.

Citizenship: a balancing act

In May 1996, the master of a Dublin maternity hospital considered it his duty to alert the nation to a problem he was encountering. Pregnant women from outside the EU were finding their way to Ireland to have their baby delivered here. Six hundred such babies had been born in that particular year. The doctor was expressing his concern about the high rate of infectious diseases such women might carry and also about the cost this practice entailed. But more was implied in this episode, for it stressed the abuse of the citizenship rule. Irish citizenship, and consequently a right of residence in any country of the EU, is automatically granted to those who are born in Ireland. The same story was revived more recently. The masters of Dublin's three main maternity hospitals reported increases in births from non-EU nationals: about 600 women from Russia, central Europe, the Middle East and Africa had come to Ireland in 1998 to have their babies delivered. Citizenship was also on the mind of some commentators on the Romanian gypsies episode. It was reported that Romanian men were hanging around girls' secondary schools, hoping to impregnate schoolgirls, in the hope that the fathering of an Irish baby would bring a right of residence!

The idea of citizenship now possesses a long history. It emerged when members of a society ceased to be considered as subjects of the ruler. Citizenship referred to the members of the political community and implied their fundamental equality, at least in relation to public authorities. All citizens of the nation-state enjoy the same rights and face the same obligations. In that sense, citizenship renders all particular identities – such as gender, race, age, religion – irrelevant. But the concept of citizenship seems to have lost this association with universal equality. It is nowadays invoked to mark the boundaries of the political community, of society itself organised as nation-state. Citizenship identifies those who enjoy rights, to the exclusion of all others. Once supposed to institutionalise all key universal values, it is now used to exclude, reject, particularise. It becomes the wall, the barrier which protects an abstract national community. Citizenship grants privileges to those who belong at the very same time as it denies them to the non-citizen. Most expressions of prejudice and intolerance, most strategies of rejection, are based on the boundaries which have been traced around citizenship. The foreigner is, by definition, the non-citizen, even if some categories of citizens are themselves estranged and fall into a second-class citizenry.

Some anthropologists have identified a principle which underlies a great deal of social life. They have pointed to rules of reciprocity according to which individuals or groups relate to each other. Any breach in this principle of reciprocity will produce rejection, hostility and enmity. The concept of citizenship contains its own rule of reciprocity. Bryan Turner[6]

---

6 B. Turner (ed.), *Citizenship and social theory*, London: Sage, 1993.

argues that citizenship should not be defined as a set of legal rights and obligations, but in terms of practices. Citizenship involves rights and duties, entitlements and obligations, all of which are fulfilled through activity. It does not simply indicate a status, but refers to a mode of participation in the group. It demands activity and achievement. Some effort is implied by political participation: the citizen endeavours to be well informed and assumes a role in the public sphere. As autonomous and self-reliant individuals, citizens perform their economic role and contribute to the common weal, as well as ensuring an adequate living for themselves. Their rights or entitlements depend on the contribution they make to society.

The five million tourists who visit Ireland every year are not seen as a problem or a threat, however unIrish their demeanour may actually be, because the economy benefits from their presence. Neither are the numerous foreign students sojourning here to learn English. EU nationals participate in a global exchange which brings Ireland into a European political and economic framework. Many, and probably most, foreign groups have found their place: the Chinese have created an economic niche for themselves in providing exotic food, while many Muslims work as medical doctors in Irish hospitals. Most such foreigners have managed to establish a balanced relationship with the people around them. But not all: asylum seekers and Romanian gypsies are not so easily integrated.

Asylum seekers attract a great deal of hostility because they are not perceived as participating in a relation of reciprocity. Doubts are widely expressed about the claims of many of these people. Seventy per cent of Irish people think that the majority of asylum seekers, claiming a status of political refugee, simply come here for economic reasons.[7] They are widely decried as 'scroungers' and 'layabouts'.

7 *Sunday Independent* poll, 9 August 1998.

All refugees do not tell a story of success and integration. For instance, only one-quarter of the Vietnamese and Bosnian adults living in Ireland have attained full-time employment. Language problems and the difficulty of obtaining recognition for their qualifications continue to exclude them from mainstream Irish society.[8] There was, from the start, a sense that asylum seekers from Romania were doomed to join the underclass. Their poor command of the English language, their lack of relevant skills and their cultural association with nomadism bode badly for their future integration into Irish society. They could not realistically balance their claims to residence in Ireland with the promise of meaningful participation. It has been contended that many asylum seekers, particularly those from Africa and Cuba, have a great deal to offer in terms of relevant skills. But they are not allowed to use such skills.

The recent prosperity of Ireland has lured many foreigners from poorer countries. They arrive, it is perceived by some, to enjoy an affluence which has been hard won and remains precarious. They face many people who, after sacrifices and cutbacks, are still to benefit from this wealth. And feelings run deep. Mary, a street-trader, lives in a place in which many refugees are lodged and she complains bitterly about them. 'They just walk in and get everything I don't get: a medical card, free rent, £64 in the pocket. They are bad neighbours: they throw their waste on the balcony, leave their children unattended. In the evening, men arrive and keep late hours.'[9] Hostility is activated by the small details of daily life, by the difficulties of cohabitation, by the different rhythms according to which different cultures live. But cost constitutes the most recurrent complaint. The fact that asylum seekers in 1998 cost the Irish state more than

8 Refugee Resettlement Research Project, *Report of a survey of the Vietnamese and Bosnian communities living in Ireland*, Dublin: The Refugee Agency, 1998.
9 *The Irish Times*, 26 May 1998.

£50 million is endlessly repeated. Even the homeless resent the 'foreigners' being granted welfare and rent allowances. A near-riot developed when refugees and homeless people were required to queue in the same welfare office for their benefits. Intolerance is not only directed at non-citizens. Some Irish citizens are themselves on the receiving end of strong prejudices. This applies to cultural minorities such as the 22,000 Irish Travellers who experience extreme hostility. Their hybrid lifestyle, half sedentary and half nomadic, has marginalised them and they have been made largely dependent on the state. Their exclusion to a large extent mirrors the fate of all those who are barred from the mean-ingful participation which goes with citizenship, for example the long-term unemployed or those on very low pay living in disadvantaged areas. They too experience prejudice because for the time being they find themselves unable to redress the balance of citizenship.

Conclusion

This chapter has argued that prejudice and intolerance towards foreigners is not related, in a fundamental way, to an Irish identity which would feel under threat. The rejection of cultural minorities erupts every time the reciprocity of social relations is breached in a significant way. The refugees, and more particularly the Romanian gypsies, have triggered hostility and rejection because they would not or could not enter into reciprocal relationships with Irish people. The response towards these groups, either hostile closure or tolerance, depends to a large extent on creating for such groups the conditions of a balanced participation in Irish society.

Learning the language appears, of course, crucial in order to avoid cultural withdrawal. The open and sensitive expression of minority cultures, as well as public displays of their cultural symbols, will bring these groups nearer the mainstream (at a time when the mainstream is itself widen-ing from within). But foremost amongst these conditions will

114

be their economic participation. A debate has actually opened about the interdiction of gainful employment which refugees face. Many voices have been raised, calling for the removal of such a rule. The organisations that represent small businesses have jumped at the opportunity and have suggested that such people would constitute a useful addition to the labour force at a time of potential labour shortages. Their economic participation would certainly establish a better balance between the entitlements and the contribution of such groups, and considerably ease the hostility which they attract. The danger remains that hostility towards them would intensify with the first signs of economic slowdown. They would then be perceived as taking the jobs of the Irish. In most European countries, hostility has increased dramatically when immigrants found it difficult to obtain work, when they had to depend on welfare, when they could no longer participate in a positive way to the life of the group. But the creation of the appropriate conditions for the balancing of entitlements from and participation in Irish society seems to be in the gift of state authorities.

CHAPTER 9

Horses and the Culture of Protest in West Dublin[1]

A. JAMIE SARIS, BRENDAN BARTLEY, CIARA KIERANS,
COLM BREATHNACH AND PHILIP McCORMACK

This chapter is an analysis of the struggle to keep horses on garden plots and on what were, until very recently, de facto commons within an economically depressed suburban environment. This struggle takes place in the face of a new regulatory regime seemingly designed to deny this area and its population any form of horse ownership. The neighbourhood is Cherry Orchard. Although scarcely five miles from Dublin's centre, it is worlds away from the centre's physical redevelopment and high street capitalism. The 5,500-strong population answers to the classic profile of a neighbourhood in trouble. It is a high crime area, with low employment rates and high rates of drug use and abuse. Cherry Orchard is seen as a prime example of the dark under-

1 This research was made possible by the generous support of Combat Poverty, the Katherine Howard Foundation, the Ballyfermot Drugs Task Force and the Ballyfermot Area Partnership. We would also like to gratefully acknowledge those individuals who, over two years, shared their lives with us and in the process provided us with some of the insights contained in this chapter. Any mistakes and/or omissions are entirely our own.

belly of urban life: squalid, drug-infested, anti-authority, welfare-dependent and crime-ridden. Not surprisingly, the area has a strained relationship with most official organs of the state: the schools, the gardaí and, perhaps most especially, Dublin Corporation.

The urban horse

As part of his analysis of the institutions of the bourgeois state, Michel Foucault examines the birth of the normalising society, which he associates with such phenomena as urbanism and the growth of the wage economy.[2] A variety of institutions emerged as part of this process to inspect and police individuals and populations, such as asylums, clinics and prisons. These institutions attempted to classify, monitor and reform individual subjectivity and behaviour. Foucault points out the phenomenon of resistance to such institutions, but does not explore resistance in any great detail. This chapter considers the resistance to a type of normalisation

---

2 M. Foucault, *Madness and civilization*, New York: Vintage Books, 1973; *Birth of the clinic*, New York: Vintage Books, 1975; *Discipline and punish. The birth of the prison*, New York: Vintage Books, 1979.

in the new Ireland, namely the attempt to police horse-ownership in Dublin and to confiscate certain animals. It will examine the interface between individual agency and structural constraints in applying and resisting state power.

Legislative background to the protest

Horses in Cherry Orchard are a symbol of identity and community ownership. Currently, substantial groups of young men and boys stand round-the-clock vigils over dwindling herds and play cat-and-mouse games with officials attempting to seize their beasts. Eager twelve-year-olds, dressed in Nike trainers and listening to West Coast rap, will, if you can find them, relate the best hiding places, while detailing who has lost beasts 'to the Corpo'. In between these adventure stories, they make longer term plans to get water and fodder for their charges.

This chapter of Cherry Orchard's existence began at the end of 1996 when, under pressure from Dublin Corporation, novel horse licensing laws were passed in Ireland. The new laws came on the back of some lurid stories concerning the supposed mistreatment of horses that live in built-up areas without the facilities to properly care for them. Concerns had also been voiced by various authorities about the dangers posed by wandering horses. These depictions tended to construct poor urban/suburban horse owners as ignorant, careless and casually brutish people. They suggested that a new regulatory regime was needed to protect both the horses and the general public.

The gist of the 1996 law is this: all horses are to be licensed and electronically tagged; and horse owners who cannot show that they have an acre of land available for their horse's upkeep (in effect all working-class horse owners in the city and the suburbs) are not able to get licences and, thus, their horses are liable for seizure. The new law also took the enforcement of these rules away from local Peace Commissioners and gave it to a private security firm contracted by Dublin Corporation.

From the beginning horse owners in Cherry Orchard felt that the law had one main purpose:

> The law they brought in now, Control of Horses 1996, it should be called 'The Eradication of Horses'. They do not want people in urban areas ownin' horses – they want horses out of Dublin. If we lived within a quarter of an inch outside Dublin, we could own a horse, you know, and they've made this law so harsh that people just can't afford the price that they're asking – £36 a day in the pound, £60–70 transport fee, £25 licence, £25 microchip . . . it's crazy.

Through most of 1997 these laws were only indifferently enforced; but fear was spreading in Cherry Orchard and Ballyfermot. There is a Ulyssian streak in many residents in these areas. They have grown up defined by, and resisting, a variety of institutions. They have had to learn their rights and entitlements in order to survive. They knew that according to the wording of these new laws, *all* horses were potentially seizable, and they felt that it was only a matter of time before they lost their beasts.

Their worries turned out to be well founded. The stringency of the new regime was slowly fuelled by regular allegations of mistreatment of city horses in the press. In November 1997, a spectacular automobile accident, involving a bus filled with school children and a lorry, occurred near the M50 roundabout. Fortunately, there were no serious injuries, but the accident was incorrectly reported to have been caused by a young boy racing his horse on the expressway. The initial report from *The Irish Times* left no doubt who was at fault; the 'true' explanation, absolving the boy on the horse, received nowhere near the same amount of column space.[3]

In 1998, the round-up began in earnest. The new regime became proactive: seizing horses, whose presence had been

3 J. Cusack and J. Humphreys, 'Horse riding youth speaks to Gardaí about bus accident', *The Irish Times*, 7 November 1997.

previously tolerated, from Corporation wasteland. The first offence against the new regulations requires a fine, which most people in these areas cannot afford; and each day that the animal is impounded, the financial impossibility of the exercise becomes ever more apparent. Thus, a law that originally looked like a simple sop to sentimental, middle-class animal lovers became yet another large social fissure around already-excluded communities. As a result the state became responsible for scores of horses: horses deemed too sick by state veterinarians have been put down, while others have died through sheer neglect (the government simply does not have the facilities to keep up with the seizures). In turn, there have been serious assaults on several enforcers of the new law, and a couple of protest marches on the Mansion House.[4]

Images of horse ownership in Dublin

Perhaps there was a certain inevitability about the battle over the symbolic and material presence of the horse in poor neighbourhoods around Dublin. Observers have long high-lighted the phenomenon of urban/suburban horse ownership in the city. *The Commitments* and other Roddy Doyle novels, along with films such as *Crushproof,* recognise the urban horse as one of the peculiar, quasi-ethnic features of Dublin working-class areas. The strength of these portrayals works on the juxtaposition of opposites – they construct horses as 'traditional' objects, only tenuously in the modern world. Middle-class people are surprised at seeing horses in poor urban settings and at how accepting the 'natives' are about encountering such animals in gardens, flats or apartment block lifts.

---

4 C. Dooley, 'Horse-owners march to highlight animal slaughter', *The Irish Times,* 11 March 1998; J. Mooney, 'DSPCA alleges intimidation', *The Irish Times,* 11 June 1996; M. O'Hallaran, 'New laws signal the end of the ride for urban cowboys', *The Irish Times,* 6 February 1998; J. Smith, 'At the end of their tether', *Sunday Times,* 15 February 1998.

Horses also summon up other bucolic images from the past, such as strong family ties and an organic community exhibiting bonds of mutual help and solidarity. Such portrayals construct these aspects of working-class life as also under threat. It is not surprising, therefore, that one can almost universally hear from horse owners in Cherry Orchard that this is their 'traditional' practice. 'Horses have always been here', 'this is the way *we* do things', and similar phrases were ubiquitous in our interviews with horse owners. Even the murals on the street proclaim that this is a 'horsey' area.

Wall mural, Cherry Orchard

On the other hand, much of the press maintains that the interest of Dublin's poor in horses is a more recent (and consequently less legitimate) phenomenon. They portray Cherry Orchard and other parts of Dublin as 'horse crazy', marking the peculiar affection that many (particularly children) feel for these beasts.[5] Despite the sympathy that many journalists express at the distress working-class children experience when losing their horses, they are also quick to point out the irrationality of this pursuit. It is as if these children are seen as the victims of a sort of mass hysteria, yet another pathology in certain socially excluded areas,

---

5 For example, J. Smith, 'At the end of their tether', *Sunday Times*, 15 February 1998.

already afflicted by drugs, broken families and domestic violence.

In 1997, the figure of 3,000 horses running more or less loose in the city became conventional wisdom amongst many commentators.[6] Despite the guesswork that went into this figure, it was repeated regularly in the media, thereby reassuring society that the 1996 legislation had been necessary to protect the health and safety requirements of a modern city.

Three thousand horses is almost certainly a recent peak in horse ownership in Dublin.[7] Nonetheless, views and reports on the horse phenomenon, from both inside and outside the community, are often disingenuous. Journalists who speak of the 'horse craze' as a recent phenomenon, severely underplay the long history of horse ownership in certain areas, and amongst some families.[8] At the same time, the local ideology of horse ownership being 'traditional' hides a great deal, not the least of which is how few families (less than 10 per cent) actually have anything to do with horses in any Dublin neighbourhood. Also, horse owners can be very different from one another: one can find animals in Cherry Orchard that look dispirited and underfed, as well as beasts that are maintained at near-dressage quality.

The current urgency around horse ownership, and its blossoming as a badge of identity, is certainly a more recent development. Horse ownership has become a symbol of resistance. The struggle around horse ownership has also become linked to Cherry Orchard's experience (and historical

6 For example, D. Walsh, 'New licensing law will have a dramatic effect on ghetto culture', *The Irish Times,* 15 August 1997.

7 Even then, we believed that this figure was an overestimate, probably designed to fan the perceived 'crisis' around horse ownership. Our best guess is that there was a maximum of 170 horses in Cherry Orchard at the start of this research in the autumn of 1997. There were certainly far fewer horses at the end of 1999 (around 40), after more than two years of stringent enforcement of the new licensing laws.

8 For example, D. Walsh, op. cit.

memory) of often oppressive official institutions, and to its current social problems, especially rapidly growing rates of opiate addiction among young people. The community is also deeply suspicious about the motives of those making decisions that affect them. To some degree at least, the background to the current horse legislation bears these worries out.

Institutional paranoia

From a certain point of view, the concern that initially motivated this new regulatory regime does seem sinister. Prior to the 1996 legislation there had been a system of laws in place to ensure the humane care of horses. It was able to impose fines, and it had provisions to impound wandering horses. It seemed adequate to its task. Locally based Peace Commissioners had a variety of means, often informal, of intervening in most situations. In turn, the locals (particularly the younger ones) tended to respect their decisions, even when they resorted to impounding.

The ethical concern over horses wandering around, when for the most part they wandered only on Corporation wasteland, is rejected by most people in the area as a credible reason for the legislation. As one of the better-known horse owners in Cherry Orchard put it:

> Progress. Yeah, the land development that's going on, like there's horses on the land all over the place and by law . . . if you're occupying a property for about twelve years, you've got certain rights to the land. Now, this is just another side of it, it may not be the reason, so if a horse is there twelve years they can claim certain rights, squatter's rights and things. So, the reason for bringing that bill in could be – a pragmatic approach to it would be to get the horses off the land – bring this law in because there's millions and millions of pounds worth of land there and these people are claiming it and they've had success getting squatter's rights 'cos horses have been there for so long. That could be another reason for

bringing in the legislation with this influx of property rises [sic] sky-high in the market. If they had started doing that building on land where there was horses before the [1996] bill, there would have been problems for them because them people would be claiming squatter's rights and entitled to do so because they've been there for the last 30 years. My father, for instance, has got purchase from that land situation over across the train-tracks. The developers who have built factories there . . . they offered him a deal to get off the land.

Some of these accusations are starting to ring true. After several boom years in Ireland, there is a very limited amount of undeveloped land, zoned for industrial use, that is convenient to Dublin's city centre. The area around Cherry Orchard and north Clondalkin, where seizures have been most intense, has also been developed at a breakneck pace. This recent construction of warehouses and factories obscures the fact that between one and two hundred horses were run on the same land only three years previously.

The current situation

The sometimes paranoid, even occasionally violent, response of certain members of the Cherry Orchard community has to be seen in context. In recent years, the community has seen major anti-police riots and militarised police raids aimed at combating the drugs menace. The largest of these, Operation Dóchas, resulted in hundreds of arrests. These raids, while potentially popular with the community, were conducted in so heavy-handed a fashion that the police largely alienated their natural base of support, that is, the majority of people who were sick of seeing junkies in their everyday environment.

By the mid-1990s Cherry Orchard was suffering from a cluster of social problems created by growing wealth disparity in Irish society, unemployment and the increased availability of heroin. Within this context, horses and the interest in horses seemed to be one of the positive aspects of living in Cherry Orchard. Although many local people saw horses as a sort of dangerous nuisance that they would be better off without, children in particular began to see that, of the limited number of roles on offer to them, one of the few positive ones was 'horse owner'. Consequently, those with horses experienced more widespread respect than had previously been the case. Some of our informants believe that this emerging sense of pride around horses, their new visibility as a marker of self-respect for folks who have historically been both erased and silenced, might actually be the main target of the legislation. They feel that people in Cherry Orchard have been obliterated from the built environment. Many residents, for example, came from politically powerless, inner-city families, and are very conscious of being turfed out in the last few decades to sometimes half-completed suburbs. Furthermore, they feel that outsiders believe that they *should* be silent, that they should feel nothing but shame for their inability to better themselves in the brave new world of the Celtic Tiger.

When speaking about horses, then, our informants move easily between oppressive legislative regimes of the past and present:

A. If you look back on the history, the only people that ever owned horses was rich people, you know, and for people in urban areas to own horses, you know, you're not supposed to 'come up in life' when you live in an urban area or you live in a council/corporation estate. You're not supposed to raise above em . . . any expectations of, you know, of anything . . .

B. It's like the penal laws . . . What was it, that if an Irish peasant had a horse that was more valuable than a lord, the lord was entitled to confiscate the horse and take it from you regardless of value.

C. Buy it for a set fee – the value of the horse, actually anybody not a member of the Established Church.

B. Under a fiver wasn't it, it couldn't be worth a value over five pound or you paid a fine.

C. Yes, they'd take it from you.

D. It's being used again as a measure, but now there's two things. Wealthy people have them, but it also, it's not appearing in the middle-class areas. It's appearing in areas which are, if you like, places like north Clondalkin, Fettercairn, even around town.

C. Where else in Dublin? In Ballymun?

D. Everywhere, Ballymun . . . it's interesting that both extremes in a sense in terms of status varies you know. Like really wealthy areas down the country have it, while other areas like . . .

B. It's upsetting the balance of relativity in our country . . . I'm sure middle-class people are saying, look, how can these people have horses, and we haven't, and we're middle class. So it's upsettin' the balance of relativity. They're coming out of their stations . . .

Horses in the balance of relativity

This sense that the conflict around horses is related to social change and class division came across in several of our encounters in Cherry Orchard. Celtic Tiger Ireland has witnessed better-off segments of Irish society gaining more in both absolute and relative terms than poorer ones. Meanwhile, Irish society has largely re-conceptualised poverty in terms of particular spaces and specific populations. The idea that 'we as a society have poor members' has pretty much given way to 'there are poor communities in our environment'. Each of these communities is now provided with an area-based 'development organisation' and 'partnership', funded largely with European money. A corporatist alliance of community, business and government is dedicated to improving life in these poverty-stricken areas. But significantly this ecological model of poverty maintains them as *separate* areas. These areas are then treated like 'national parks' that contain the potentially dangerous forces of the socially excluded. They are watched over by socially-designated 'rangers' such as specially trained police, social welfare officers and community development workers. These professionals both maintain the boundaries around, and keep the peace between, the natives. In Cherry Orchard, some of the natives ride bareback.

Cherry children and their horse

All the 'socially excluded' suburbs of the Dublin fringe, for example Fettercairn, north Clondalkin, Cherry Orchard and Ballymun, have recently completed or are currently building (under the auspices of community development) equestrian centres. These centres are to provide jobs for locals and a focus for youth, other than drugs and crime. Such projects, however well intentioned, tend not to be able to accommodate the very elements most concerned with the loss of their horses, that is, young socially excluded males. Therefore, despite the enlightened effort to put in place facilities to care for horses locally, troubles ensue.

One example of this tension in Cherry Orchard is the straightforward issue of how many horses will eventually be housed in the new equestrian centre, the Integra Project. Even the highest estimates of the capacity of the new facility are far fewer than the number of horses in the area. This leads to a potentially fatal game of musical stable places that some elements in Cherry Orchard believe they are being set up to lose. But, there is an even touchier subject: who should control the new structure? The whole picture is complicated by the fact that many of the most vocal protestors – those wanting to overturn rather than to accommodate the new regulations – are connected to wilder, even criminal, elements in the locality. However, even those who only dabble in trouble tend to see the community groups behind the centre as a middle-class imposition on their everyday life, rather than as allies in 'developing' themselves or their community.

These young men, generally with guidance from some of their older compatriots, are the ones making the most visible protests, hiding and moving their horses for weeks on end, and occasionally resorting to violence. This resistance to the regulation (and disappearance) of horses is then constructed in the media as an irrational attachment to useless animals, yet another problem with ghetto culture and one more handicap dragging this population away from successful participation in the market economy. In turn, this strengthens the symbolic importance of horses within the community, and they become all the more important and worth fighting for. They become a marker for 'our' territory and a stake in a struggle with 'them'.

A major meeting at the end of 1998 between the community group officials connected to the centre and the boys and young men most concerned with the situation quickly deteriorated into a shouting match. An eleven-year-old boy summed up the general feeling of the audience: 'we love our horses, and we want OUR horses on OUR fucking land, not Bal-fuckin'-briggan, County-fuckin'-Meath' (an alternative equestrian centre suggested as at least temporary housing for those beasts not able to be accommodated at the new centre). This is the crux of the matter. It is this 'OUR' that is being contested with horses, both within the community and between the community and the outside world. In this way, horses provide one of the main cultural shapes for the experience of social exclusion in this area of Dublin, as well as serving as specific cultural resources through which the violence associated with such exclusion is resisted. In the process, this resistance highlights the existence, and some of the nature, of the power being exercised against this area and population.

CHAPTER 10

Carnival Ireland

MICHEL PEILLON

I want to put forward an unusual idea: an idea that does not come naturally to mind; that is not part of a shared understanding of the world; that plays, as yet, no obvious ideological function; and has no wide currency among intellectuals. This idea can be stated simply: societies produce more resources than they require, and this excess of resources becomes a serious problem for them. This line of thought has been developed by Georges Bataille, in a book entitled *The accursed share*.[1] Groups and societies are faced with the problem of 'consuming' a surfeit of resources. This excess will generate turbulence and effervescence if it is not absorbed into further growth. Surplus resources must be disposed of, dissipated in an unproductive way. War, religion, luxury, spectacle and festivity all represent forms of unproductive expenditure on which the group may rely.

The idea that affluence (meaning that which is surplus to requirement) is bound to create difficulties will find many resonances in Ireland. I suppose it constitutes the fundamental assumption of puritanism. It lurked behind de Valera's vision of a frugal and contented rural Ireland. The

---

1 G. Bataille, *The accursed share. An essay on general economy*, Volume 1, New York: Zone, 1988.

regular denunciation by the Catholic Church of the growing or rampant materialism also reflects this deep suspicion about the presence of such a surplus. The newly found affluence of the late 1990s has itself aroused some concern about the possible impact of the new wealth. In the past, Ireland has dealt with the 'accursed share' by adopting a religious kind of unproductive expenditure. It has supported a large and well-off religious class, multiplied holy days during which work was not allowed and established numerous religious festivities. This chapter will argue that festivities now constitute a major form of unproductive expenditure: Ireland's way of lifting the curse of affluence. It also examines another way Ireland has of celebrating its achievements: how, for instance, a myth has been elaborated around Mary Robinson, who has come to enjoy the status of an unofficial hero of modern Ireland.

From craic to carnival

Wunenburger contended that festivities are pulled between two poles.[2] The Apollonian pole promotes ceremony and control, while the Dionysiac pole generates frenzy, extravagance and effervescence. Most observers of Irish festive occasions in the eighteenth and nineteenth centuries have pointed to their boisterous nature. Wren parties were often rowdy affairs, while the Biddies processions showed little respect for the saint they were promenading. Rules about drinking and courting were clearly relaxed in May-Day gatherings. Midsummer and harvest festivities also occasioned excess. Even pattern days in the recent past experienced drunkenness, licentiousness and violence, which definitely transgressed the established norms of behaviour.

Such practices have been curbed and slowly eliminated. The pressure from both secular and religious authorities has

---

2 J. J. Wunenburger, *La fête, le jeu et le sacré*, Paris: Jean-Pierre Delarge Editeur, 1977.

134

stamped out the boisterousness of festivities. The latter have, during the twentieth century, rarely threatened the canons of morality. The reversals of the established order, in which a wild interregnum was set, have been tamed into charity events or simply commercial occasions. The plunge into anomie, from which social order is supposed to come out stronger, was no longer allowed. The main celebrations remain very much under control. The processions of Corpus Christi in the recent past, the parades of St Patrick's Day or even Halloween bonfires hardly endanger public order.

The festive feeling revived somewhat in the early 1970s when many localities initiated various festivals. Attracting tourists or even weekend visitors emerged as a routine strategy of community development. Any town worth its salt organised a festival, any kind of festival. This systematic promotion of festivals is justified as a way of supporting the local trade and placing the town on the map. Bord Fáilte keeps an up-to-date list of such festivals on its website. The commodification of festivities transformed them into strategic and utilitarian occasions, and this drastically altered their nature. Participation in such events became discretionary and a mere matter of consumption; festivities had been transformed into a kind of leisure activity.

A sense of fun has been added recently to the list of ingredients that go into making a marketable 'Irishness'. Other ingredients include heavy sociable drinking, conversational wit and affability. All these features have come together to form what some cultural entrepreneur has labelled 'craic'. Craic indicates the conviviality and playful banter that develop around a drink in the pub. It stresses features that are deemed both endearing and unique to Ireland and functions as a term of celebration. It suggests that, in this peripheral and struggling country, people have managed to retain a balanced attitude to life. In an age of despondency, they have salvaged a form of good life. But this rather introverted celebration of Ireland is being displaced by the fiesta and the carnival: crowds, movement, rhythm, colour. The fiesta and the carnival now constitute the celebratory mode of an assertive and confident Ireland. An Ireland which takes its place in the world; an Ireland which leaves its mark; an Ireland which wants to make a lot of noise.

The decision to start the Tour de France in Dublin was rightly interpreted as a compliment paid to Ireland. It represented, of course, a tribute to the exploits of Stephen Roche and Sean Kelly in international cycling. It was also a way of signifying the closeness of Ireland to mainstream Europe and France. As the preparations got under way, the event was presented in a purely utilitarian light: it would give Ireland the kind of publicity money cannot buy. Officialdom pointed to the benefits to be enjoyed. The government had from the start paid a subsidy of over £2 million, but local authorities incurred further expenditure. Wicklow County Council spent £1.5 million resurfacing roads, while 500 gallons of paint were slapped onto buildings along Waterford's quays – not to mention the 10,000 flowers planted in County Wexford. Altogether, £6 million was spent on improving the Tour roads. Against that, the anticipated revenue of the Tour in Ireland was estimated at around £30 million. And this did not include the huge media coverage offered by the occasion: close to one billion people would, in the 163 countries where the race was broadcast, have the opportunity to admire the rich scenery of Ireland. The utilitarian emphasis was further highlighted when the Dublin Chamber of Commerce and the Small Firms Association expressed concern about the adverse effects of traffic restrictions on the retail trade in Dublin.

However, the attempt to justify the Tour de France on utilitarian grounds quickly became irrelevant. The Tour coming to Ireland was not a matter of money, of counting costs and benefits, it was a cause for celebration. Stephen Roche retorted to the critics: 'it is going to be mayhem; but it is worth it'. And people took the view that, in fact, it was this mayhem which made it worthwhile. Around the spectacle of the Tour, with its long publicity caravan preceding the race, towns and villages decided to initiate their own festivities. They were going to throw a mighty party. Hundreds of parties.

They competed in organising festive events and endeavoured to outwit each other. Vintage car rallies, pig derbies, all kinds of sporting events, angling displays, busking competitions, puppet shows, karaoke concerts (the biggest in Europe), circus acts, jugglers and stilt walkers, parades and historical pageantry, mardi-gras costumes, fashion shows, floral displays, pet shows, craft and art exhibitions, fireworks and laser displays, street barbecues, food fairs, French cuisine tasting, displays of threshing and butter-making. And of course music and dancing, sometimes all-night long: jazz bands, brass bands, pipe bands, numerous concerts featuring popular singers, midsummer balls, ceílís, waltzing competitions, set dancing and so forth. Ireland had simply decided, in the heart of the summer, to give itself a grand fête, on a scale not experienced for a long time. The Tour de France had ceased to represent a way of making money for Ireland. The meaning of the event had been diverted and turned into a spectacle for its own sake, a festival for the fun of it.

Towards the end of August 1998, another opportunity for celebration offered itself. The Cutty Sark Tall Ships Race was arriving in Dublin. The attention of officials again turned to the economic side of the affair. While the hosting of the event would cost £1 million, a spending bonanza of £30 million was announced. But, once more, the event was transformed into large-scale festivity. One million people from all over Ireland thronged to Ringsend to admire the mighty sight of the sailing ships. The names of the tall ships echoed exotic places: *Libertad, Guauhtemac, Orsa Maggiore, Mir,* and *Mloziezy.* The enthusiasm of the crowds lifted the occasion to a fully-fledged festival: four days of fun and celebration, with musical events, street-theatre and dancing. The festival was crowned by a parade of the tall ships sailing in Dublin Bay.

Another peak of celebration was reached when a five-day millennium festival was organised around St Patrick's Day 1999 in Dublin. The spirit of the exercise was well caught in President Mary McAleese's official greeting of the event: 'I have no doubt that it will be a wonderful celebration of our country, our culture, our sense of community, our sense of fun – all those things that make us proud to be Irish'. And the crowd responded in mass to the call.

The celebration started with a fireworks extravaganza. On an unseasonably balmy night, Dubliners transformed the event into a large-scale festivity, into a fiesta that they offered to themselves. Perhaps more than a celebration, the fireworks display became a challenge, a way of showing that Dublin was not easily outplayed. Dublin was treating itself, for the whole world to see. The spectacular half-hour display had been commandeered from a leading pyrotechnician from Australia. He had organised displays for the Atlanta Olympic Games, the handover of Hong Kong to China and New Year's Eve in Sydney harbour. The grand dimension of the event was well advertised: the cost paid by the sponsor, the six tons of fireworks, over 15,000 shells, the elaborate preparation and organisation. It was pure spectacle, a display of conspicuous consumption on a large scale. But it was also a statement of power: of that very special kind of intangible power where competitors outdo one another by the sheer dissipation of wealth, by a grandiose display of luxury through which a reputation is established.

The fiesta went on for several days, thereafter with a clear focus on street-theatre and carnival, to culminate in the St Patrick's Day Parade. Troupes had been brought in from Togo, Cuba, Catalonia and, indeed, Galway. The taste for popular fiesta, with its extravagance, colourful costumes, rhythms and dancing, is growing in Ireland. Some of these troupes have been involved in conducting workshops with local schools and youth groups. It is hoped that their skills as street-performers will be handed down and that a new generation of Irish people will successfully animate carnival pageants. As quintessential festivity, the carnival brings people together as participants in a spectacular event. They enter into a whirlwind of colour, costume, movement and playfulness. Through it, and for no other purpose than the enjoyment of the day, the group dissipates some of its wealth and a great deal of its energy.

138

The President's feats

Ireland does not celebrate itself only through festivals and carnivals. In a more symbolic way, it can also produce heroes through whom it projects a positive and idealised image of itself. 'There is an atmosphere of irresistible fascination about the figure that appears suddenly as guide, marking a new period, a new stage, in the biography', wrote Joseph Campbell in his classical analysis of the hero.[3] Mary Robinson came to attract such a fascination and marked a new stage in the history of Ireland. Heroes are constructed around myths, that is to say around narratives which bear little relation to observable reality: they exist in order to carry a meaning. The construction of Mary Robinson into a hero is not simply a question of personal biography, but a way of defining contemporary Ireland, or more to the point of celebrating Ireland. Let us narrate the tale of the myth that has developed around Mary Robinson.

A hero represents a person of exceptional gifts, sometimes honoured by the group of origin, sometimes unrecognised and disdained. One is told that these exceptional gifts manifested themselves when, still in her early twenties, Mary Robinson obtained the Reid Professorship of Law at Trinity College. She was also, soon after and quite surprisingly, elected to the Seanad. But promising qualities do not make heroes. They are forged through the challenges they face and the ordeals they undergo. The young senator showed her mettle by taking on the Catholic hierarchy and challenging the church on the very grounds it was most determined to protect, those of personal and family morality. She came to represent the liberal agenda, pushing for legislation on contraception, divorce and resisting the imposition of a fundamentalist agenda on abortion.

The story unfolds further. As a candidate in the presidential election, she was thought unlikely to displace the

---

3 J. Campbell, *The hero with a thousand faces*, New Jersey: Princeton University Press, 1949, p. 55.

Fianna Fáil grip on this honorific and inconsequential position. When she won, she became not only the first female President of Ireland but, more essentially, the symbol and the public face of the new Ireland. But the ordeal had still to be faced: against the pettiness of Irish politicians, intent on marginalising a potential competitor, she confronted the task of overcoming the absolute powerlessness of such a position. This was achieved by a skilful reliance on symbolic acts. She visited marginalised communities and groups, for example Travellers, women's groups, gay people, and she invited them into the presidential home. She stood as the friend of Protestants in the Republic, and then reached out to the most marginalised communities in nationalist Northern Ireland. 'The effect of the successful adventure of the hero is the unlocking and release again of the flow of life into the body of the world.'[4]

She embodied Irish modernity, to the world and to the Irish people themselves; but she did not let herself become imprisoned in the image she had forged for herself. Although she contributed to the demise of the Catholic Church on the issue of 'sexual' morality and attracted the hostility of many, she enjoyed a quasi-unanimous approval rating as President. She came to symbolise an Ireland that was confidently taking its place in the world: one that had achieved recognition. She represented an Ireland from which the gloom was seemingly lifting. And this modern Ireland did not reject the past or exclude tradition: all could celebrate this Ireland. Mary Robinson was the medium of this celebration; or rather, Ireland celebrated itself through its President.

The story is not fully written yet. Mary Robinson, the much-sung hero of Ireland, departed to greater tasks and glories. She announced that she would not seek re-election and would move to the high-profile international position of UN Commissioner for Human Rights. The marginalised

---

4   J. Campbell, *The hero with a thousand faces*, New Jersey: Princeton University Press, 1949, p. 40.

groups, in which 'the flow of life had been released' by President Robinson – community groups, youths, Travellers, gays, the homeless – launched a general invitation to a popular street party in front of the GPO in Dublin, to pay tribute and to say thank you. The festivities were planned for 6 September 1997, but they were engulfed by the emotional outpouring in the aftermath of Princess Diana's death. The expected street party actually fell on the day of Diana's funeral. Festivities were marred and the popular tribute cancelled.

The celebrations faltered, but the myth did not. On the international scene, Mary Robinson has faced other challenges and met other ordeals. And she has made Ireland proud by the image she presents to the world: her principled defence of human rights; her refusal to compromise; her struggle against the inertia and ineffectiveness of international organisations. Or so the media tells us. The celebration of her achievements and of the feats to come – for nobody doubts that she will perform such feats – was simply deferred.

Conclusion

People have, in the last few years, eagerly joined in the celebration of Ireland. They have acknowledged what has been achieved and manifested their satisfaction at the happy turn of events. They have done so mainly by their willingness to transform certain public events into special festive occasions and to embrace the exuberance of the carnival atmosphere. This has happened for the Tour de France, the Tall Ships Race and St Patrick's Day. But these occasions have also been turned into ostentatious displays and dissipations of wealth and energy. They were underlined by a latent competition, one in which the reputation of localities and the very image of Ireland were at stake.

The desire to celebrate the new Ireland has also been expressed in the making of heroes. A public figure such as Mary Robinson has come to stand for attitudes and values with which many people could identify. She has symbolised a break with the old ways and the failures of the past. Not only has she been seen as projecting a positive image of Ireland abroad, but she has also formed one of the vehicles through which Ireland could think of itself in positive terms.

The enthusiasm for festive occasions and the making of heroes represent two of the ways through which Ireland is redefining itself. There is no reason to believe that the newly acquired collective confidence and mood will undermine whatever critical spirit may be found here. On the contrary, this celebratory disposition will raise the standards on which Ireland's achievements are judged. It will also thrust into the public sphere the contentious question of how best to use the new wealth. This brings us back to Bataille, to the difficult task that society faces in disposing of such wealth, in eradicating the 'accursed share'.

CONTESTED REFLEXIVITY

CHAPTER 11

The President's Communion

RICHARD O'LEARY

On Sunday 7 December 1997, President Mary McAleese, a Roman Catholic, received Communion in a Protestant cathedral in Dublin. This action was in breach of the Catholic Church's teaching on inter-church Communion. The Catholic Church forbids Catholics from receiving Communion from a Protestant minister, and it does not generally allow Protestants to receive Communion from a Catholic priest. This was believed to have been the first time that an Irish President of the Catholic faith had taken Communion in a Protestant church. The President's Communion was photographed and made front-page news in the national newspapers.

There was an immediate negative public response from some prominent Catholics. Monsignor Denis Faul emphasised that Catholic Church laws applied to the President as much as to any other Catholics. A senior academic, Fr James McEvoy, declared that he would find it 'repugnant if she should ever again abuse the august office which she occupies, in a way which would once more embarrass the Catholic Church, by giving scandal to its members'.[1] There was a flurry of commentaries in the newspapers and numerous

---

1 *Irish News,* 12 December 1997.

letters from the public, notably in *The Irish Times*. The following week the Catholic Archbishop of Dublin, Dr Connell, used the word 'sham' in a radio interview when describing Catholic participation in Communion in a Protestant church. While the Archbishop afterwards insisted that his precise use of the word 'sham' in this context was misunderstood, it nevertheless inflamed the controversy. A spokesman for the Catholic bishops said of the President's action that it 'took everyone by surprise' and that 'it is hoped that the issue will not arise again'.[2]

We can interpret the President's Communion, and the practice of inter-church Communion generally, as a challenge to traditional Catholicism, within an increasingly questioning and pluralistic Irish society. The challenge to tradition in modern society has been understood by Anthony Giddens in terms of 'reflexivity' and an emerging 'life-politics'.[3] Giddens describes the reflexivity of modern social life whereby social practices are constantly examined and reformed by individuals in the light of incoming information. Among the concerns of life politics are issues of self-identity. Individuals are increasingly adopting a critical attitude to traditions and to authorities, and in so doing re-create their own self-identities. We will trace the origins from which the challenge to traditional Catholicism on the issue of Communion derives in Irish society.

The challenge to traditional Catholicism

The participation in inter-church Communion by the President and others could be viewed as a struggle over what types of Catholics, and Christians, they want to be. Letters to the newspapers at the time of the controversy suggested that these Irish Catholics wish to forge an identity which is ecumenical to an extent that is much greater than

---

2   *The Irish Times*, 16 December 1997.
3   A. Giddens, *The consequences of modernity*, Cambridge: The Polity Press, 1990.

that envisaged by the official teaching of the Catholic Church. The forging of this identity may be facilitated by the assertion of cultural rationality. In the first volume of this series, Michele Dillon referred to the cultural rationality associated with modernity. Cultural rationality can be present when 'people use a common-sense approach grounded in their own experiences rather than the authority of elites to determine what is important and what is less central to religious identity'.[4] In this way, Irish Catholics can broadly believe in Catholic dogma but reject particular teachings as being unreasonable in practice.

Another source of the challenge to traditional Catholicism has emerged from the reforms within the Catholic Church. Since the Second Vatican Council (1962–65) the Catholic Church has given increased recognition to the place of the individual Catholic conscience, even if it still stresses that this conscience should be informed by church teaching. Michael Fogarty claims that this has influenced Irish Catholics in a number of ways.[5] By 1981, he noted a shift across generations from stronger to weaker acceptance of orthodox beliefs and religious practice and of the authority of the church.

In the doctrine developed during the Second Vatican Council (Vatican II), the Catholic Church also gave increased recognition to the other Christian churches. This signalled its desire for ecumenism, worldwide Christian unity, a desire that is shared by the main Protestant denominations in Ireland. Vatican II also gave a stimulus to theological thinking generally. Out of this have emerged some theological voices which dissent from official Catholic teaching on issues including inter-church Communion. The credibility of the

---

4   M. Dillon, 'Divorce and cultural rationality', in M. Peillon and E. Slater (eds.), *Encounters with Modern Ireland*, Dublin: Institute of Public Administration, 1998, p. 129.
5   M. Fogarty, 'Report on the survey', in M. Fogarty, L. Ryan and J. Lee (eds.), *Irish values and attitudes: The Irish report of the European value systems study*, Dublin: Dominican Publications, 1984, p. 12.

official Catholic teaching on Communion is likely to have been weakened by the growing number of dissenting theological voices, such as that of the prominent Catholic theologian, Fr Enda McDonagh. The stimulus that Vatican II gave to theological thinking generally was not confined to the clergy. In the decades since, increasing numbers of lay Catholics have become theologically literate and have participated in the formulation of church thinking, especially on pastoral matters. Mary McAleese, prior to becoming President, was one of these devout and yet questioning lay Irish Catholics.

Both Communion in their own church and inter-church Communion appear to have taken on a new meaning for Catholics in recent decades. Among those Catholics who attend Mass, there has been an increase in the receipt of Communion. In the Republic of Ireland in 1974, when 91 per cent of survey respondents reported that they attended Mass weekly, only 28 per cent of them received Communion.[6] In 1988/9, although weekly Mass attendance had fallen slightly to 82 per cent, weekly receipt of Communion had grown to 43 per cent.[7] Furthermore, a positive attitude to inter-church Communion has developed. This has been articulated by Fr Gabriel Daly who said that: 'Roman Catholics may find – and an increasing number do find – that receiving Communion at the Eucharist of another tradition carries deep meaning for them, and they can think of no convincing theological reason against doing so'.[8] It would also appear that on the issue of inter-church Communion, opinion at the popular level is much more positive than that at the official or episcopal level. In a nationwide poll in the Republic of Ireland, 60 per cent 'totally agreed' with the decision of the President to receive Communion in the Protestant church.[9]

6 A. Breslin and J. Weafer, *Religious beliefs, practice and moral attitudes*, Maynooth: Council for Research and Development, 1985.
7 M. MacGréil, *Prejudice and tolerance revisited*, Maynooth: Department of Social Studies, 1996, p. 170, table 55.
8 *The Irish Times*, 22 January 1998.
9 *Prime Time*, RTÉ, 3 February 1998.

The formulation by some individual Catholics of a new view of the practice of inter-church Communion is also being influenced by their reflections on inter-communal relations in Ireland. This is especially so in the context of the peace talks. This influence can be detected in the very development of the ecumenical movement in Ireland. Ecumenism has been boosted in Ireland by the political impetus to respond to the outbreak of religious group violence in Northern Ireland. Many churchgoers wanted to challenge sectarianism and attending ecumenical services was one practical response they could make. It is evident that some Catholics, in the light of their knowledge of inter-communal conflict, are bringing new thinking to bear on the traditional practice of Communion. For example, Fr Enda McDonagh has proposed that Catholics should be encouraged to join in the Eucharistic celebration of other churches as a manifestation and a means of developing reconciliation between Christians.[10] Some evidence that McDonagh's view is shared by others is found in the arguments of letters sent to the newspapers at the time of the Communion controversy. Indeed some commentators have attributed this to the President as a motive for her action.

The social basis to the challenge to traditional Catholicism

It is not just that Irish Catholics are increasingly questioning the traditional teaching on Communion, but that there are increasing opportunities to give effect to their changing beliefs. Prior to 1966 Catholics were banned from attending Protestant religious services. It is striking to recall that in 1949, at the funeral of President Douglas Hyde, a predecessor of Mary McAleese, the Catholic ministers in government had not even dared to enter the Protestant church. In the aftermath of Vatican II, the Irish Catholic hierarchy ended

---

10 E. McDonagh, 'Invite and encourage', *The Furrow*, vol. 50, no. 1, January 1999, pp. 18–25.

its ban and thereby greatly facilitated the actual meeting of Catholics and Protestants in situations of worship. From the late 1960s, annual ecumenical services for Christian unity and for peace in Northern Ireland were introduced in many parts of Ireland. From a situation of no joint worship we note that, by 1984 in the Republic of Ireland, 18 per cent of Catholics reported that they had attended an ecumenical service.[11] While it is not usual to have Communion available at a formal ecumenical service, at least some of these persons are likely to have been exposed to the opportunity and to have participated in inter-church Communion. Ecumenical contact may also be leading some Catholics to reflect upon their Christian identity and to conclude that inter-church Communion is not wrong, despite the teaching of their church.

Although the extent of its occurrence is not known, it appears that inter-church Communion is not an exceptional practice. There is evidence, from the reports of individuals in their letters to newspapers at the time of the President's Communion controversy, that inter-church Communion has occurred before. There is documented evidence of inter-church Communion occurring among intermarried couples in Ireland in the early 1980s.

The increase in the number of intermarriages is the other source of increase in the opportunity to participate in inter-church Communion. Intermarried couples now number about 10,000 couples in each of the Republic of Ireland and Northern Ireland. While up to the early 1970s, inter-church wedding ceremonies were usually solemnised in the Catholic Church, since then ceremonies in Protestant churches have become increasingly common. This development reflects the relaxation of Catholic Church rules restricting the solemn-isation of intermarriages anywhere other than in a Catholic Church. At these wedding ceremonies, and at baptisms and funerals, Catholics may find themselves in situations where

---

11 A. Breslin and J. Weafer, *Religious beliefs, practice and moral attitudes*, Maynooth: Council for Research and Development, 1985.

they can participate in Communion in a Protestant church. The Protestant churches are generally welcoming in this regard. A survey, conducted by the author in 1995, of recent intermarried couples in Dublin, found that about one in three of the Catholic partners had received Communion in their Protestant partner's church in the preceding twelve months. Overall, the fact that inter-church Communion is not an exceptional practice is consistent with our interpretation of it as reflecting underlying changes in Irish society.

Tony Fahey describes how the Catholic Church had fostered a sense of Catholic distinctiveness using religious doctrine and ritual to maintain boundaries between Catholicism and the world around it.[12] Vatican II reformed both religious doctrine and rituals which weakened those boundaries. Reforms of ritual in both the Catholic Church and the Church of Ireland have narrowed the outward appearance of differences between these churches. More active lay participation in the most important Catholic ritual, the Mass, was recommended by Vatican II. This led to the transformation of the Mass from a service performed in Latin to one conducted in the vernacular and thus reduced the distinctiveness of the Catholic form of worship compared to that of Protestant denominations. The form of service in the Church of Ireland has also changed to become more like that found in Catholic churches. This is evident in the increasing use of candles, and in particular votive candles, during worship, the wearing of albs and colourful stoles, the adoption of a common Eucharistic prayer and the use of the revised common lectionary. From the point of view of ordinary Catholics, Catholic and Church of Ireland Communion services are becoming less and less distinguishable.

The attitudinal gap between some Catholics and some Protestants on matters of morality has been narrowing since the 1970s. Not only did doctrinal, ritualistic and attitudinal

---

12 T. Fahey, 'Catholicism and industrial society in Ireland', in J. H. Goldthorpe and C. T. Whelan (eds.), *The development of industrial society in Ireland*, Oxford: Oxford University Press, 1992.

differences between Catholics and Protestants narrow but, as we saw above, inter-group contacts developed rapidly after the mid-1960s. This convergence appears to have weakened for many Catholics their sense of separateness from Protestants, and is likely to have facilitated a new thinking about, and openness to, participation in inter-church Communion.

Conclusion

We have attributed the emerging practice of inter-church Communion to a challenge to traditional Catholicism, by an increasingly questioning Irish Catholic public. A growing number of individual Catholics are formulating their own position on inter-church Communion, and one which is contrary to the official teaching. They are articulating an ecumenical Christian identity, which is informed by their own consciences, their ecumenical contacts and their desire to improve inter-communal relations in their country. They are given opportunities to participate in inter-church Communion by the growing number of occasions when Catholics and Protestants worship together. According to this interpretation, the issue of, and conflict surrounding, the practice of inter-church Communion is not a one-off controversy but is likely to arise again.

CHAPTER 12

Talk Radio

SARA O'SULLIVAN

The majority of Irish people listening to radio in the mornings listen to a talk radio show on either RTÉ Radio 1 or 2FM. Talk accompanies the routine activities of these listeners and is the backdrop to work both in the home and in other settings. Talk radio is seen to complement news and current affairs output and so to contribute to RTÉ's public service brief. The morning talk radio shows on RTÉ Radio 1 feature the usual suspects, most typically representatives of political parties, interest groups or other organisations, being interviewed about the news stories of the day. In contrast *The Gerry Ryan Show* and *Liveline* feature a mix of light and serious topics and the majority of the speakers are ordinary people rather than experts.

Talk radio shows allow access to listeners; they can provide a forum, albeit a restricted one, for democratic debate and discussion. It is this aspect of the genre that many writers have studied. A key component of talk radio shows is callers' stories about themselves and their everyday lives. Perennial topics include health, sex, relationships, parenting and so on. On *The Gerry Ryan Show*, which has a tabloid style, these everyday topics might be punctuated by people ringing in to talk about being abducted by aliens, about Daniel O'Donnell or about the size of their bottoms. These are all human-interest stories and are often dismissed as entertainment. However, an alternative way of looking at this talk is to consider the role that story-telling plays in the life of an individual and of a society.

According to Giddens, in the modern world the self becomes a reflexive project, that is something to be reflected upon and changed by the individual on an ongoing basis. The key to this project is the stories that we tell about ourselves and our biographies. 'A person's identity is not to be found in behaviour . . . but in the capacity *to keep a particular narrative going*', that is to sort events into a coherent story about the self.[1] Talk radio shows facilitate the development of reflexive self-identities by providing a space for listeners to tell their stories. In addition, listening to debate and discussion on talk radio shows can provide the audience with information that enables their individual reflexive projects.

From silence to openness

In an Irish context, talk radio has provided a valuable space for issues around sexuality and self-identity to be explored. I will focus on this aspect here, although talk about relationships and bodies are equally central. Originally, British and American television shows and movies brought sex into Irish homes. More recently, Irish media such as *The Late Late Show,* the *Sunday World* and talk radio began covering more risqué topics. Irish commentators have emphasised the role that talk radio has played in relation to recent changes in Irish society. Although a number of negative newspaper articles about the genre have been published in recent months, writers here have been largely positive about talk radio. Their focus has been on the impact of sexual stories, 'the big story' of the late twentieth century. The value of the genre is seen to rest in the forum it offers listeners to talk about issues that were once taboo.

---

1 A. Giddens, *Modernity and self-identity: Self and society in the late modern age*, Cambridge: Polity Press, 1991, p. 54.

It has been argued that telling sexual stories on Irish talk shows is progressive, liberating and educational.[2] Topics previously confined to the confessional began to be talked about in public. Callers rang Irish talk radio shows to tell stories about their personal lives, to talk about their marriages, sex lives, relationship problems and so on. These stories did not erupt spontaneously or out of a vacuum. As Ken Plummer puts it, they were 'modernist stories . . . stories whose time has come'.[3] In Ireland, the time of these stories came later than in Britain or the US. Their emergence can be linked to the decline in the power of the Catholic Church in Ireland. Part of the secularisation process involved a renegotiation of sexual identities. The Catholic Church and the Irish media offered competing versions of what constituted 'normal' sexuality. An increase in talk about the intimate sphere is unsurprising at a time when new modes of behaviour are under negotiation.

These sexual stories were of political significance, given that over the last twenty years major political issues have centred on the private sphere. Issues of family and sexuality were the battleground for the struggle between church and state that characterised this period. Talk radio provided a space where issues such as abortion and divorce could be discussed by those with direct experience of them. This was a change from the usual experts, politicians and members of the clergy, who were wheeled out to speak in current affairs debates elsewhere on RTÉ. So, unlike American television talk shows, which tend to focus on 'deviant' sexuality, it is 'normal' sexuality and sexual relationships that have been opened up to outside scrutiny by Irish talk radio.

Talk radio shows have also provided a space where

---

2 See, for example, R. Fletcher, 'Silences: Irish women and abortion', *Feminist Review*, vol. 50, 1995, pp. 44–66; P. O'Connor, 'Understanding continuities and changes in Irish marriage: Putting women center stage', *Irish Journal of Sociology*, vol. 5, 1995, pp. 135–63.
3 K. Plummer, *Telling sexual stories: Power, change and social worlds*, London: Routledge, 1995, p. 120.

survivors can bring the powerful to task. This process involves the telling of a different type of story, the survivor's story. Survivors of child abuse, rape and domestic violence have used talk radio to voice their experiences in order to demand justice. This has had consequences for the survivors themselves, for the audience and for those held accountable: 'sensitizing the public and politicians to the issue of extreme child abuse, the need for accountability, and above all justice'.[4] Talk radio has provided a space for these stories to be told and so has had a role to play in forcing the private experiences of Irish women and children into a very public arena. Rather than acting as a substitute for the sacrament of confession, these survivors have used talk shows to declare not that they are sinners, but that they have been sinned against.

However, talk about sex is not necessarily emancipatory. Problems do not automatically become easier to solve just because they have been named. A persistent focus on the individual and individual stories can be seen as problematic, in that it works to obscure structural factors. While the personal is the political, talk about the personal must lead to political action if change is to occur. Stories become very tired when the emphasis is on personal rather than political change. The demands put on us by talk radio hosts to tell our sexual stories and to keep nothing secret may be as problematic as the old orthodoxies we have rejected.

The good fight against traditional Ireland was sexy for a number of years, and therefore made good radio. However, the talk radio shows on Radio 1 have moved away from talk about sex, particularly since the 1995 divorce referendum. The talking points during 1998 and 1999 on *Liveline* were property prices, traffic, tribunals and other political scandals. Although *The Gerry Ryan Show* has dealt with these topics on occasion, the show remains focused on the everyday world. Discussions about when it is appropriate to have sex, with whom, how, and where, are continuously recycled. What has

4   H. Ferguson, 'Protecting children in new times: Child protection and the risk society', *Child and Family Social Work*, vol. 2, 1997, p. 231.

changed is the significance of this talk about sexual practices and mores. These stories may still facilitate the production of individual reflexive narratives. However, as the topic becomes increasingly predictable, such story-telling seems unlikely to play a role in any collective renegotiation of sexual mores. Instead, these tales work to support a particular view of what is acceptable sexual behaviour. This view is informed by a libertarian discourse, but is inherently conservative.

The price of talking

An important issue to consider here is the impact of commodification processes. Commodification is a central component of modernity. Giddens talks about the reflexive project becoming commodified, that is 'packaged and distributed according to market criteria'.[5] This process positions the listener in the role of consumer. Although RTÉ is a public service broadcaster, the majority of its revenue comes from advertising. Talk radio shows are seen by advertisers to offer access to an audience in control of much of the family's disposable income. The 1998 Joint National Listenership Research figures show that two of the five most popular Irish radio programmes are talk radio shows that allow access to listeners. *The Gerry Ryan Show* comes in at number 3, with 387,000 listeners. *Liveline* is just behind at number 4 and attracts an almost identical number of listeners (386,000). The 1999 rate cards reflect the popularity of these two shows. The cost of an advertisement on *Liveline* rose by 10 per cent in one year; a 30-second advertisement in September 1999 cost £592. The daytime advertising rates on 2FM increased by 18 per cent; at the time of writing, a 30-second advertisement during *The Gerry Ryan Show* cost £315. I estimate that these two shows have the potential to generate over £70,000 in advertising revenue for RTÉ each week.[6]

5 A. Giddens, *Modernity and self-identity: Self and society in the late modern age*, Cambridge: Polity Press, 1991, p. 198.
6 All figures from www.medialive.ie.

A consumerist discourse permeates a tabloid talk radio show like *The Gerry Ryan Show*, no matter what topic is under discussion. The show is in the business of selling lifestyles to its audience. The key question is whether this framing works to limit collective self-awareness to a series of lifestyle choices. To return to Giddens, he argues that reflexivity and commodification are not mutually exclusive. This is one of the dilemmas of the self that he identifies. His argument is that, although talk about sex can become predictable and standardised as a result of commodification, it nonetheless remains part of the reflexive project of the self. However, I think that he underestimates the tension between reflexivity and commodification. I also wonder whether such predictable talk might not work simply to confirm what the audience already knows, rather than enabling reflexivity. There would also appear to be a point beyond which market criteria may have a negative influence over the reflexive project. The following hoax that was perpetrated on *The Gerry Ryan Show* illustrates one possible consequence of any requirement to be entertaining.

The chain gang / page three girls hoax

A woman from Cavan rang *The Gerry Ryan Show* in January 1999 to ask advice about her authoritarian husband. He would not let her go to a strip show in their local pub, although he himself planned to attend a similar event. This story was irresistible to the production team from the outset. The caller cleverly drew on the culture clash between old and new Ireland, the staple of the genre in the past. As she put it herself, 'the men still think that the women should be living in the Dark Ages'. The show returned to this topic several times over the following weeks, lapping it up. The story got more and more convoluted with more and more details added during subsequent calls. All of which contributed to a picture of a sexually dysfunctional marital relationship, where sexual pleasure was the husband's exclusive right.

Eventually, it was revealed that the call had been made

160

as a publicity stunt by the owner of the pub where these strip shows were due to take place. Some of his friends had engaged in this elaborate role playing in order to gain some free publicity for the pub. Predictably, the producers of *The Gerry Ryan Show* were outraged, while everyone else had a laugh at their expense. There was considerable irony in the producer's reaction to the hoax. Willie O'Reilly, the executive producer of the show, argued on *Soundbyte* that the team were annoyed that they had been tricked into promoting a 'tawdry' strip show. Of course, this was far from the most salacious topic covered by the show in recent months. In addition, the show is routinely permeated by promotions, advertisements and public relations. Promotions are obviously not a problem so long as it is RTÉ that is cashing in. The final point is that the show has been responsible for some hoaxes itself in the past. Many of these were done in the name of entertainment and so seen as 'a laugh'. *The Gerry Ryan Show* regularly broadcasts scripted letters, presented as letters from listeners, to generate calls to the show. The show is entering dangerous territory once the lines between fact and fiction are blurred in this way. It seems rather disingenuous to be playing the trust card when the tables are turned.

This incident reveals that listeners can learn how to sell a story to the production team. The instigator of the hoax explained on *Soundbyte* that he listened to the show every day and that he knew it was 'that sort of a show'. His familiarity with the show meant that he knew the ingredients that would make the production team salivate. He was also familiar with the libertarian discourse favoured by the show and recognised the need to frame the story accordingly. While the producers may fancy themselves as transgressors, they are tied to an outdated notion of traditional Ireland which was exploited by the hoaxers. This hoax points to one consequence of the commodification process. It becomes unimportant whether a story is true or false as long as it is provocative and entertaining. All that matters is that the audience keeps listening.

Conclusion

Talk radio can provide a unique space for reflexive identities to be explored. However, given that the reflexive project is always subject to market criteria, the possibilities offered by the genre are ambivalent. Talk radio becomes much less significant, sociologically speaking, when it becomes a forum merely for titillation and role-playing. The recent hoax perpetrated on *The Gerry Ryan Show* illustrates this point nicely. Of course, there is always the possibility that new stories about sexual practices and self-identity will emerge, and that talk radio will have another heyday. However, as long as the same old topics continue to be rolled out it would seem that the genre exists primarily to deliver listeners to advertisers, a role it continues to fulfil very successfully.

CHAPTER 13

Information Overgrowth

MICHEL PEILLON

Modern individuals know about the world, about what is happening elsewhere. They seek and receive information about what does not really affect them. This gathering of information represents the duty but also the inclination of those who define themselves as modern. Being informed, and ostentatiously so, operates as a marker of modernity. Bruno Latour has remarked that 'the reading of the daily newspaper is the prayer of the modern man'.[1] Information was once organised, framed according to an ideology that facilitated its interpretation. We are now confronted with a mass of information that is largely unprocessed and not easily organised into knowledge.

Volumes of the 1996 census of population have been produced to give a detailed statistical profile of people residing in Ireland. The census of population constitutes a regular feature of collective life. Very few countries nowadays would fail to undertake such an exercise. One may think of good reasons why the rulers of a territory felt the need for, or the necessity of, establishing how many people inhabited their realm and also what kind of people they were: war and

---

1 B. Latour, *We have never been modern*, New York: Harvester Wheatsheaf, 1993, p. 9.

Sixty per cent of all students surveyed had smoked cannabis.

Irish students take more drugs than the European average.

Survey finds high smoking and drinking among teenagers.

The number of teenage drug abusers receiving treatment in greater Dublin has more than tripled since the start of the decade.

Alcohol-related illness, accidents and absenteeism cost the exchequer more than £325 million annually.

Addicts in the Republic being treated for drugs are the youngest in the EU.

More than 130 people died from drug dependence between 1985 and 1996.

Irish parents are deluding themselves about the extent of their children's drinking.

Children from deprived areas are much more likely than others to end up in court.

Crime rates drop by 14 per cent, but rapes and kidnaps increase.

A third of armed robberies are aimed at petrol stations.

More than 70 per cent of defendants who appear before the courts are from Dublin's most deprived districts.

The average District Court defendant is a 24-year-old man charged with stealing property.

taxation were most likely on their mind. But in the process the census has become the mark of the advanced states. Or rather, the lack of a census signifies archaism. The scope of statistical information that is produced by Ireland about itself has been widely extended beyond the regular census. Vital statistics are now routinely published, as are all kinds of economic indicators. The Household Budget Survey has turned into a major statistical exercise in its own right; using a large representative sample, it records in a precise way how Irish households spend their money.

The modernity of a country is manifested by its ability to provide relevant information to various international organisations. The number of blank lines in the reports of such organisations as the International Labour Office or the Organisation of Economic Co-operation and Development gives a negative measure of modernity: of the inability of countries to generate detailed information about themselves. Eurostat statistics bear witness to the striving of peripheral European countries, such as Portugal, Greece, Spain and Ireland, to assume the full status of members of this most modern club of nations, and to demonstrate their ability to provide the relevant information about themselves.

The promise of information

Society will know itself. It will become active and transparent. It will understand its internal workings and change itself at will. It will anticipate problems and plan ahead for their solution. Information will throw light on those dark corners of social life. The promise of information represents, of course, another version of the story of the Enlightenment. In his severe analysis of Ireland's failure to develop, Professor J. J. Lee placed the blame squarely on the unenlightened inclination of the political and administrative elite.[2] He pointed to the fundamental anti-intellectualism that characterises such

2 J. J. Lee, *Ireland 1912–1985. Politics and society*, Cambridge: Cambridge University Press, 1989.

Hundreds of Irish juveniles are locked up in conditions of extreme violence, with little access to regular education or exercise.

The Irish abortion rate in 1995 was 8.5 per cent of all pregnancies.

The majority of women who have crisis pregnancies continue with them.

The number of births outside marriage exceeded one in four in 1997.

Calls to the child sexual abuse helpline rose by 42 per cent last year.

Thirty-one per cent of women reported childhood sex abuse.

Childline got over 750,000 calls in a decade.

Twenty per cent of women are abused, before marriage, by their future husbands.

The number of reported rapes increased by 39 per cent last year compared to 1996 figures.

Women managers still being paid less than men.

Irish women gain most from education.

The number of distress calls received by refuges for battered women and their children increased by 25 per cent last year.

95,000 people in the state have experienced marital breakdown.

elites, and took as a measure of this failure the low level of information and knowledge that Ireland generates about itself. This is clearly revealed, he asserted, by the low level of development of social sciences.

Ireland now produces extensive information on itself. However, this production of information follows a logic that does not conform to the scenario of increased transparency. Not only is the production of information a source of conflict, but it reproduces a fundamental structure of inequality. For there is information and information. One type is obtained through surveys and censuses: it is gathered about people who are easily subjected to an administrative gaze. This information requires that individuals be transformed into objects. Another type of information relates to people who, because of their status and power, are not so easily scrutinised. They protect themselves, with layers of rights, regulations and injunctions, against any kind of gaze. They remain subjects in this world, able to specify the conditions under which information about them is made available.

Scandals have multiplied about the financial transactions of politicians, the ability of some people to dodge taxes with the complicity of banks. Information about such activities was so deeply entrenched that it required the creation of special tribunals of investigation. The McCracken Tribunal was set up to look into money that was paid by Dunnes Stores to Charlie Haughey and Michael Lowry. It was followed by the Moriarty Tribunal, whose brief was to inspect offshore bank accounts – Ansbacher accounts – widely thought to be used by wealthy individuals to evade taxation. The story unfolded further when one hundred employees of the National Irish Bank appealed against a High Court ruling that they must answer questions put to them by the inspectors probing into the bank's affairs. More recently, the Flood Tribunal has investigated allegations of local government corruption. It was initiated following revelations that a then minister, Ray Burke, received £30,000 in cash from a building firm in 1989. In all such cases, significant information could only be accessed through a tortuous legal process.

Fewer than 1,700 people have applied for the total legal dissolution of their marriages.

The number of births in the third quarter of 1997 was the highest figure for ten years.

Reported rapes were up by one-third in 1998.

Irish women are worse off than in sixteen industrial states.

Irish pupil–teacher ratio is the highest in EU.

Irish teachers are among the highest-paid in the developed world but work some of the shortest hours.

Report shows disadvantaged are still rare at university.

Unemployment is the number one concern of Ireland's youth.

Parents add to stress of exam students.

Twenty-six per cent of students who entered third-level education had not gained any qualification.

Forty-four per cent of pupils in inter-denominational schools are raised as Catholics.

More than 50 per cent of second-level students in Ireland associate beef consumption with increased risk of contracting CJD.

Data do not support the common perception of the Irish education system as internationally 'first-class'.

Protestants feel strongly about the Catholic decree on mixed marriage.

Not only is the production of information socially patterned, but it follows a paradoxical logic that contradicts the optimistic scenario of the information society. Far from societies, groups and individuals becoming more transparent, accrued information may have the opposite effect. An inflation of information does not uphold the reflexive orientation, it smothers it. The accumulation and systematic diffusion of information participates in a struggle against reflexivity. It forms a standard strategy in a war of attrition. This strategy was relied upon during World War I, when 'the Committee on Public Information . . . discovered in 1917–18 that one of the best means of controlling news was flooding news channels with facts, or what amounted to official information'.[3] Jean Baudrillard tells the story of the multinational oil company, Exxon. After a catastrophic oil spillage in North American waters, the US government demanded that this company report on its activities in the world. The company produced twelve volumes of a thousand pages each; it would have taken several years just to read the full report, and even more to analyse it. Any prospect of a critical evaluation of Exxon activities had been suppressed by the sheer accumulation of information.[4] More prosaically, the strategy of not informing by providing too much information is often used in relation to labels for packaged food, which feature long listings of often obscure names for ingredients.

Information and control

In a lecture he gave at the Pontifical University of Rio de Janeiro in 1973, Michel Foucault traced the rise of the survey as an administrative instrument.[5] Surveys were undertaken

---

3 E. S. Herman and N. Chomsky, *Manufacturing consent. The political economy of the mass media*, Vintage, 1994, p. 23.
4 J. Baudrillard, *Les stratégies fatales*, Paris: Bernard Grasset, 1983, pp. 17–18.
5 M. Foucault, 'La vérité et les formes juridiques', in M. Foucault, *Dits et écrits*, Volume II, Paris: Gallimard, 1994.

Travellers marry younger and die younger.

Ninety-eight per cent of those seeking refugee status enter the state illegally.

Refugees lack jobs, English and are isolated.

Travellers in West Limerick are concerned about the low number of children who go on to second-level education.

Study finds increasing violence used in suicides.

Ireland has experienced a fourfold increase in suicide since 1990, mainly young men.

The number of people who ended their own lives increased in 1997.

In 1997, 355 men committed suicide, compared with 78 women.

Males under 24 years are seven times more likely than females to kill themselves.

Male drivers are more prone to distraction than female drivers.

More than a quarter of road deaths were pedestrians in 1997.

Ireland has some of the most dangerous roads in the EU.

Ireland has the most road deaths in Europe per one thousand vehicles.

Some 80 per cent of Dublin business people who drive to and from work have seen their travel times increase in the last six months.

when the sovereign had to solve a problem and wanted to keep an eye on the wealth, feelings and behaviour of subjects. The survey was seen by Foucault as a management device, as a way of exercising power. But he also added, perhaps as a kind of afterthought, that the survey constitutes a way of validating truth, of producing something which can be considered as true. It represents in that sense not so much a mechanism for the production of information, as a way of certifying information. Information assumes the form of a survey in order to be validated as truth. This may explain why the information conveyed by surveys never gives a sense of surprise: we already knew that, but now we are sure. Furthermore, the actual reporting and communication of this information is highly ritualised. It inevitably uses the word poll or survey in an explicit way. It is always attached to some established or official body in order to carry some weight. It includes some quantitative statement – preferably in the form of a significant percentage.

The production of information through a survey also participates in the power/knowledge nexus that has been emphasised by Michel Foucault. The call for information is often rooted in a desire to classify and file. It aims at categories of people who are perceived as problematic in some way. One need not ponder too long on the ulterior motive of the Cork county councillor who called for the establishment of a national register of travelling families. A survey was undertaken by the Eastern Health Board to spot people 'at risk': it identified 233 'eccentric vulnerable adults' in the greater Dublin area. For the purpose, of course, of caring for them! Another survey established that 10 per cent of prisoners in Mountjoy Prison suffer psychiatric illness. In all such cases, the relevant information was aimed at upholding a normalising practice, cataloguing those people who must be subjected to caring, therapeutic or special administrative practices. Even the request to set up a national project to determine the extent of domestic violence against women may be construed in such terms.

A study to determine how many people aged 50 to 69 have diabetes is to be conducted.

Irritable bowel problem affects one in five adults.

Fifty-six per cent of people have personal life policies.

Lung cancer deaths are much higher in Dublin.

Survey shows fall in farm incomes.

Of the 13,500 farms in County Mayo, only a small percentage were economically viable.

Rural areas have worst suicide rate.

Rural areas continue to decline, while towns and cities are growing.

Forty-six per cent of people go to work by car.

There has been a serious decline in the population of western parishes.

Twenty-seven thousand farming households are living in poverty.

Attendance at Mass has fallen from 70 per cent to 60 per cent in the past four years.

Fermanagh Protestants feel uncertain and insecure.

Twenty per cent of gardaí have severe job-related stress.

Up to one-third of people in a survey in Derry had mental health problems.

The moral agenda

Information is an expensive commodity. It is mainly produced by surveys which involve complex and costly procedures. Either paid for by public or private funds, such surveys are somehow linked with the concerns of particular groups in society. 'In order to generate meaning, information must comply with the ever-present imperative of being moralised', notes Baudrillard.[6] The production of information becomes a crucial stage in the setting of the moral agenda. This occurs in two complementary ways. Those with a moral agenda sponsor the production of relevant information. Or else the production of such information is justified in terms of its relevance for the concern of the population or some group within it. In that way, information contributes to the construing of various practices into social problems.

The production and diffusion of information is mainly used in Ireland to express concern, raise alarm or even denounce some practices. So, which problems are constructed through the production and diffusion of information? Drug taking has been most clearly defined as a social problem, chiefly in relation to young people. This has been extended to alcoholism and it is even asserted that Ireland experiences a particularly acute problem in this context. The increase in criminality is highlighted by various statistics, and sometimes explained by social deprivation.

The family has long since been invested with a fundamental moral quality, which is nowadays perceived as seriously undermined. Endless information about the abuse of children and spouses keeps this issue high on the moral agenda. But the family is also seen as disintegrating through marital breakdown and divorce. Concern is expressed about education in Ireland and its deficiencies and shortcomings are invariably emphasised.

The increased level of suicide in the recent past, chiefly

---

6   J. Baudrillard, *A l'ombre des majorités silencieuses. La fin du social*, Paris: Editions Denoel/Gonthier, 1982, p. 15.

Visitors to Dublin complain about difficulties with crossing the road, illegally parked cars and fear for personal safety.

Ireland has the highest proportion living in poverty after the US in the industrialised world.

Thirteen per cent of visitors to Temple Bar are turned off by stag/hen parties from ever visiting the capital again.

More than 1.4 million people (43 per cent of the population over three) told the census takers they could speak Irish.

Survey finds grocers take risks with chilled foods.

Ireland is heading the world for the phosphate content of its soil. Ireland has the most rubbish in Northern Europe, with plastic waste massively worse.

Minimum wage would hurt business.

The number of people at work has reached the highest level recorded in the history of the state.

Immigration to Ireland has reached record levels.

Survey finds 44 per cent of school-leavers find jobs in a year.

More than one in ten people in the Republic have lived abroad for at least a year, usually in Britain.

Graduate unemployment has reached a new low.

The number of indictable crimes reported last year was 10 per cent down on 1996.

among young men, is steadily chronicled. The number of deaths on Irish roads is presented as a growing problem. Finally, figures are mobilised to illustrate the decline of rural, Catholic Ireland. In all such cases, information is imparted as a way of raising issues, of creating a sense of what is right and what is wrong. It possesses a strong normalising intent.

Celebration and identity

Through the production and diffusion of information, celebration also takes place. The reversal of all those features according to which Ireland was deemed a failure is endlessly recorded. The unrelenting increase in the number of people at work is emphatically noted. School-leavers find jobs speedily; graduates are easily absorbed into the labour force. Previous generations of Irish migrants are coming back home in numbers, reversing the emigration trail. The steady increase in affluence hides a multitude of sins, but it is never-theless there to be celebrated.

The celebratory character of such information is reinforced by the way it is shaped. Its dramatic significance is under-pinned by a reference to some kind of standard that has been improved upon or, even better, by a record which has been set. 'Immigration to Ireland has reached record levels', it was announced at a time when immigration still referred to returned migrants and not yet to asylum seekers. 'The number of people at work is the highest recorded in the history of the state.' Or else information points to the steady progress towards some significant standard. One needs to recall the collective elation at the announcement that Irish per capita income would soon exceed that of Great Britain. Or that before long, Ireland would have made up the gap with Europe to reach the average level of affluence enjoyed in the EU.

In a way, this kind of information is always concerned with identity, or more precisely with Irish identity. The celebration of present-day Ireland extends to 'the kind of

Tourist numbers are up by 10 per cent.

The population is at its highest level in the history of the state.

The total number of people at work increased by a record 95,000 between April 1997 and April 1998, and the unemployment rate is the lowest in recent years.

The tourist sector now employs 50,000 people. This represents an increase of 20 per cent in two years.

Women are entering the workforce twice as fast as men.

Ireland ranks seventeenth on UN index of 175 countries on the Human Development Index.

A national pilot project is going to be set up to determine the extent of domestic violence against women.

More than half of Irish people see themselves as racist, but this is significantly lower than the two-thirds of Europeans who do so.

Seventy per cent of Irish women say they have not time to make love. However, 45 per cent do manage it once a month, while an energetic 8 per cent claim to do it every day.

Only 22 per cent of the 750,000 dogs in the Republic are licensed.

A quarter of all drivers are regularly breaking the speed limit.

A clear majority of the electorate supports Mr Quinn to be the next Labour Party leader.

people we are'. That 'a quarter of drivers are regularly breaking the speed limit' implies strong individualism. This systematic breaching of rules is also invoked in the statement that 'only 20 per cent of the 750,000 dogs in the Republic of Ireland are licensed'. But then which people have ever defined themselves as conformist and compliant to authority? The finding that 'more than half of Irish people see themselves as racist' is not easily fathomed as a statement about identity. The minutest and apparently most trivial bit of information refers back, at least in a latent way, to a complex agenda. It carries with it a range of connotations. The somewhat playful statement that '70 per cent of Irish women say they have no time to make love' thrusts us back to the many threads of the Irish past: the power of the Catholic Church, the repression of sexuality and so forth. And these are stories of identity.

Assigning agency

'Almost £250,000 was spent by various Government Departments last year on determining what the public think.'[7] We may note with some interest that those who represent and govern us need to contract out surveys in order to know what we think. But more significant is the assumption that the public actually think, or even have views. Information is generated through polls and surveys that sample broad categories of people. They seem to give a voice to a mass of people who otherwise would have none. This kind of information constitutes a way of assigning agency: of defining a mass of people as a source of genuine meaning. It confers a quality of autonomy and choice to categories of people who demonstrate no such intent or uphold no such attitudes.

Many polls and surveys are engaged in the highly ideological exercise of creating agents: that is to say of entities which prove capable of deciding, choosing and acting. When

---

7 *Sunday Tribune*, 21 February 1999.

Most voters believe that the Budget will favour those on high incomes.

Seventy-seven per cent say limited abortion right should be provided.

New survey reveals strong growth of optimism among Irish business.

Seventy-five per cent of those polled are satisfied with the way the Taoiseach, Mr Ahern, is leading the country.

Ninety-one per cent believe health professionals should be obliged to report cases of child abuse.

Eighty per cent of nationalists support the Orange Order's right to march, provided parades are well marshalled with no flags or military emblems displayed and no controversial tunes played.

Eighty-two per cent of Irish voters have no view on the Amsterdam Treaty.

Ninety-four per cent agree that religious education should continue to be included in the primary school curriculum.

There is no clear consensus among people in Northern Ireland on a single political outcome.

Eighty-four per cent of people feel there is an urgent need for emergency accommodation and crisis intervention in hospital.

More than 80 per cent of people want banks to be prosecuted for fraud.

masses are tested and polled, they are given a kind of life. 'Everywhere one tries to have the masses speak, one presses them to exist in a social, electoral, syndical, sexual way.'[8] Agents which are so constructed fulfil, in their very inertia, a useful purpose. They formulate an opinion that becomes public by the mere process of its aggregation. They embody a purposeful public, which acts as a kind of alter ego to the political class and confers legitimacy. For this political class has only to remain within the confines of a predictable public opinion in order to find its political action validated, justified. Baudrillard argues that public opinion is not only a message: it also constitutes a medium, the channel through which validating opinions are reproduced and publicised.[9]

Sometimes this assigning of agency acquires a phantasmagoric quality: '82 per cent of Irish voters have no view on the Amsterdam Treaty'. The public is here constructed as a caricature of agency, devoid of intent or purpose. Or else it is emphasised not that the budget will favour those with high incomes, but that: 'most voters believe so'. It is difficult to resist the fascinating insight into the Northern Irish situation that was provided by a particular survey: 'there is no clear consensus among people in Northern Ireland on a single political outcome'. One may also be perplexed by the regular polls that announce the popularity rating of various political leaders. The figures indicating the proportion of people stating their approval of the leader of a party for which they do not vote appear particularly intriguing. This particular logic reached its climax when it was declared with great seriousness: 'a clear majority of the electorate supports Mr Quinn to be the next Labour Party leader'. Yet, 80 to 90 per cent of those who answered the poll have never voted and will never vote for the Labour Party. Public opinion has

8   J. Baudrillard, *A l'ombre des majorités silencieuses. La fin du social*, Paris: Editions Denoel/Gonthier, 1982, p. 28.
9   J. Baudrillard, *Symbolic exchange and death*, London: Sage Publications, 1993, pp. 101–2.

More than 60 per cent of Irish people believe it is reasonable to send refugees back to the EU country to which they first arrived.

Suicide and traffic accidents were the main causes of death in cases coming before Dublin City Coroner's Court.

Forty-three per cent of people in Dublin use a taxi once a week.

One in three women will be physically molested, says expert.

A recent survey of life insurance coverage shows that only 56 per cent of respondents have personal life policies.

attained an apex of irrelevance. But in the process it projects the public as agency.

Conclusion

Sometimes information is produced which possesses no purpose. It acquires an incantatory quality, in which the production of statistics and the carrying out of survey polls is transformed into a ritual of modernity. What can we make of the information that '43 per cent of people in Dublin use a taxi once a week'? The meaning of this statement is not found in the information it imparts, but in its vacuity. This kind of information has become absolutely redundant, it has lost any meaning, it has destroyed its signification. We have reached the stage of informational delirium, when information floats freely in a sea of insignificance. It means nothing, it signifies nothing, it refers to nothing. It stands on its own, as information in its purest form.

CHAPTER 14

Irish Democracy and the Tribunals of Inquiry

MARY P. CORCORAN AND ALEX WHITE

In recent years, the tribunal of inquiry has become something of a fixture in the national consciousness. It is mediated through the extensive coverage afforded the cumbersome proceedings on radio, television and in the national newspapers. As the proceedings unravel at a snail's pace, we are treated to the peaks of explosive revelation and the much more frequent troughs of turgid testimony. The public gallery is filled on a daily basis with 'ordinary citizens', anxious to catch a glimpse of the major players bringing others to account, or more interestingly, being brought to account themselves. The tribunals have made celebrities out of ordinary citizens; James Gogarty's tetchy interventions and sound bite ripostes to counsel have rapidly diffused into the public arena as 'gogartyisms'. Denis McCullough SC was lionised for his steely staring down of a former Taoiseach who was once thought to be invincible. Tribunal exchanges are nightly re-enacted on national radio by professional actors for the broader public; an exercise in the acting out of democracy. It seems therefore apposite to pose the question as to whether or not the rise of the tribunal and its penetration into civic life heralds a new era of deliberative democracy.

According to Jürgen Habermas, deliberative democracy

reflects a concern that citizens' participation in the democratic process ought to have a rational character; that participation in democratic politics should be predicated on public discourse constituted through informed argument on a range of general interests.[1] In other words, deliberative democracy is a process through which all members of the group decide, in all equality and on the strength of the best argument, how the group should live and what goals they should pursue. Do tribunals facilitate such a deliberative process or do they simply offer up another illusion, a spectacularised version of democratic process?

The form and function of the tribunal

The Tribunals of Inquiry Act, 1921, is a British statute which allows for the establishment of a tribunal 'to inquire into matters of definite public interest'. But the conceptualisation of what is in the public interest seems to be remarkably fluid. While there is no consensus on how it should be defined, the notion of what constitutes public interest seems to have evolved over time. Definitions run the gamut from loss of confidence in the institutions of state to the idea of exposing an evil, or determining that an evil has not, in fact, transpired. The Irish Supreme Court has tended to follow the judgment of the *Report of the Royal Commission of Tribunals of Inquiry 1966* in the UK (the Salmon Report) which argued that inquiries 'should always be confined to matters of vital public importance concerning which there is something in the nature of a nation-wide crisis of confidence'.[2] The Salmon Report, however, falls short of providing clear indices for adjudicating what type of matter might be of the magnitude of 'a crisis of public confidence':

---

1   J. Habermas, *Between facts and norms: Contributions to a discourse theory of law and democracy*, Cambridge: Polity Press, 1996, p. ix.
2   P. Gallagher, 'Tribunals and the erosion of the right to privacy', Paper presented at Bar Council of Ireland Seminar on Inquiries: The Rights of Individuals, Privacy and Confidentiality, 17 July 1999, p. 1.

> It is essential that on the very rare occasions when crises of public confidence occur, the evil, if it exists, shall be exposed so that it may be rooted out; or if it does not exist, the public shall be satisfied that in reality there is no substance in the prevalent rumour and suspicions by which they have been disturbed.[3]

The Irish Supreme Court employs an equally broad formulation in suggesting that tribunals have a function in relation to 'matters of urgent public importance *when inquiries are necessary to preserve the purity and integrity of public life*'.[4] The maintenance of high standards in public life is crucial to the public interest. The tribunal's deliberations must allay public scepticism and disquiet on the issues that led to the establishment of the inquiry in the first place. Hence the importance attached to setting out clear terms of reference to which the inquiry must confine itself. Indeed, in the considerable case law generated by the tribunals to date, the most notable feature has been the emphasis placed on procedural propriety. For the tribunals to succeed, adherence to correct procedure in the context of the terms of reference is paramount.

According to Brady, the demand for a public inquiry:

> . . . has become part of a new culture where Tribunals have taken the place of State agencies and statutory bodies in investigating alleged wrong doing by politicians. An aspect of rule by government is now being replaced by rule by tribunal. Statutory agencies such as the Revenue Commissioners and An Garda Síochána are being relegated, by this cultural change, to a secondary role. Tribunals have in reality, become a new political art form.[5]

3 P. Gallagher, ibid., p. 2.
4 D. McGrath, 'Review of Moriarty Tribunal and Flood Tribunal to-date', *The Bar Review*, vol. 4, no. 5, 1999, p. 234.
5 R. Brady, 'Reflections on Tribunals of Inquiry', *The Bar Review*, vol. 3, no. 3, 1997, p. 121.

There seems to be some truth to this assertion. In the 1990s there has been a rush to establish tribunals. Is there more evil abroad, or have we just become more scrupulous about identifying it, exposing it and excoriating it? The pillars of Irish society are shaken while the quest for accountability extends itself to the very heart of the state. Although the legislation underpinning tribunals dates from 1921, the vast majority of tribunals have occurred only within the last twenty-five years and, most particularly, since the mid-1990s. Despite their varied remits, they share a common focus:

- The interrogation of facts (including expert systems).
- An emphasis on transparency (tribunals are nominally open to all citizens and receive regular coverage in the press and electronic media).
- The subject matter necessitates self-confrontation by witnesses to the tribunal (the focus is on the how and why a particular state of affairs came to pass).

The rationale for the tribunals is straightforward: people are entitled to know why certain events took the course they did. As a corollary, there is tacit assumption (as yet untested) that conducting a tribunal can achieve some kind of closure on an event, obviating the risk of a repetition of that event in the future. In the 1970s, there was a tribunal of inquiry into the Stardust Disco fire in which many young people lost their lives. In the 1980s, tribunals were convened to examine the Kerry Babies case and the Whiddy Island oil disaster off the coast of Cork. In the 1990s, we have witnessed a succession of tribunals, including the investigation into the beef industry; the tribunal of inquiry on the transmission of hepatitis C/blood products contamination; the McCracken Tribunal on Dunnes' payments to politicians; the Moriarty Tribunal on payments to Charles Haughey and Michael Lowry; the inquiry into planning in North Dublin chaired by Mr Justice Flood; and the recently convened tribunal of inquiry on haemophiliacs/blood products contamination chaired by Judge Alison Lindsay.

There is no doubt that in one particular regard the more recent tribunals are distinctly different in their terms of reference to those convened in earlier decades. In the 1970s and 1980s, the tribunals were established as agents of the state to inquire into the how and why of some (external) event that had adversely affected an individual or set of individuals within the body politic. Since the establishment of the Beef Tribunal, the remit of the inquiries has focused much more specifically on the internal workings of the agencies of the state, and the day-to-day business of government. Indeed, one senior counsel has described the proliferation of tribunals as a response to 'an obsession with investigating the past'.[6] It is the whole process of governance itself and the relationship between government and its citizenry that has come under scrutiny in recent years. This turning inward, this evaluation of the conduct of the servants and power brokers of the state indicates that the tribunal of inquiry is an institution that is rooted in reflexive modernisation. The certitudes that went before, the taken-for-granted nature of everyday life in Ireland, are deconstructed daily in the tribunal. In this sense, the tribunal is an ostensibly modern institution that embodies one of the preoccupations of modernity: the need to stand back and engage in a reflexive interrogation of the self.

But, paradoxically, the tribunal also lacks reflexivity because it is afforded no power to be prescriptive, to outline a normatively based strategy for how society and, in particular, the public interest might be better served. The deliberations of the tribunal remain just that – deliberations. Any subsequent criminal prosecution of a citizen must proceed without recourse to material uncovered in the course of the tribunal. In a sense, the tribunal and its proceedings, having been seen to serve the public interest, are hermetically sealed.

---

6   R. Brady, 'Reform of the Law of Tribunals', Paper presented at Bar Council of Ireland Seminar on Inquiries: The Rights of Individuals, Privacy and Confidentiality, 17 July 1999.

Other regulatory institutions such as the Garda Síochána, the Law Courts and the Revenue Commissioners are embedded in the machinery of the modern bureaucratic state, and are, therefore, empowered to both deliberate and act. In contrast, the tribunal is more ephemeral in character. It neither springs from the public sphere nor is it embedded in the institutions of the state.

The practice of tribunals

As Mr Justice Flood recently reiterated, 'tribunals are factual inquiries into how certain events came to take place and why they took the form that they did'.[7] In other words, a tribunal performs first and foremost an inquisitorial rather than an adversarial function. It is investigatory and interrogative. 'It is pre-eminently a finder of fact. It does not determine rights, duties or obligations. It has no power to impose a criminal conviction or to adjust legal rights.'[8] A tribunal undertakes five stages of inquiry:

1 A preliminary investigation of the evidence available.
2 The determination by the tribunal of the relevance of that evidence to the particular matter under inquiry.
3 The service of evidence on those relevant to the inquiry.
4 The public hearing of witnesses and their cross-examination.
5 The preparation of a report and the making of recommendations based on the established facts.

The increasing popularity of tribunals as a way of getting to the 'true facts' suggests that formal rather than substantive rationality is the engine driving the process forward. Weber distinguished between formal rationality (in which areas of life are organised on the basis of rational calculation) and substantive rationality (in which goals and values are given

7 *The Irish Times*, 5 August 1999.
8 R. Brady, 'Reflections on Tribunals of Inquiry', *The Bar Review*, vol. 3, no. 3, 1997, p. 122.

greater significance). Weber was aware of the inherent tension between both forms of rationality in modern society, just as he was sensitive to the opposition between bureaucracy and democracy. He understood that the growth of the modern bureaucratic state proceeds in close connection with political democratisation. The demands made by democracy for political representation and legal equality require complex administrative and juridical provisions to prevent the abuse of power.[9] By virtue of their terms of reference, however, the provisions of the tribunals of inquiry tend to privilege formal over substantive rationality. As Weber predicted, a gulf opens between factual and ethical truth. The tribunals are pre-occupied with the accretion of facts. 'Messy' issues, such as morality and moral judgements, must be bracketed for the duration of the inquiry. Normative orientations, which might lead toward the application of a more substantive rationality, and in turn a more deliberative democracy, are for the most part eschewed.

The transparency function of the tribunal, to lay bare the facts, is limited. A key theme that regularly percolates to the surface in the tribunals is the potential conflict of interest between respect for the private life and affairs of the citizen and the tribunal's remit to provide for a public inquisition of the activities of the citizen. Despite the fact that under the terms of the Tribunals of Inquiry Act, 1921, the public are, in principle, entitled to be present at any of these proceedings, in practice the courts have taken the view that the public are entitled to be present only at the fourth stage outlined above. This is because in weighing up the right to know of the public with the right to privacy of the citizen under investigation, the courts have taken the view that the right to privacy is paramount. It is even possible to exclude the public (and the media) from the fourth stage, when evidence is being given by a witness, if the chairman of the tribunal deems the exclusion to be appropriate. This was the case, for example,

---

9   A. Giddens, *Capitalism and modern social theory*. Cambridge: Cambridge University Press, 1971, p. 180.

in the taking of evidence from Joseph Murphy Sr in the Flood Tribunal proceedings. Both the public and the media were excluded from his deposition. Video link-up was also disallowed by the tribunal's chairman. The restriction of public and media access further undermines the capacity of the tribunal to play a role in creating a more deliberative form of democracy.

Re-visiting the issue of public interest

According to Pat Rabbitt TD, 'A Tribunal of Inquiry can effectively inquire into matters of public interest, make findings of fact and it is a matter for Dáil Éireann – although effectively for the government – to decide, what action, if any, is warranted'.[10] The tribunal, then, is constituted by the Oireachtas and is ultimately accountable only to the Oireachtas. It remains a creature of the state rather than an instrument of the public sphere. Similarly, it falls considerably short of the status of a court of law. As was pointed out earlier, the tribunal is not embedded in the ordinary deliberative institutions of the state. No judgments or decisions can emanate from the tribunal since it is confined to unearthing facts rather than engaging in normative evaluations. In the case of *Haughey* v *Moriarty* (28 July 1998), the Supreme Court endorsed its earlier decision, in *Goodman* v *Hamilton* ([1992] 2IR542), that a tribunal is not engaged in the administration of justice.[11]

These prescriptions on the role and function of a tribunal demonstrate its essential limitations as an instrument of deliberative democracy. Whatever agency the tribunals may exercise in terms of their inquisitorial and fact-finding role, there is at present no possibility of moving from being merely the legally constituted conscience of the public to being

---

10 P. Rabbitt, 'A Tribunal of Inquiry or an investigation by Dáil Committee?, *The Bar Review*, vol. 4, no. 3, 1998, p. 114.

11 D. McGrath, 'Review of Moriarty Tribunal and Flood Tribunal to-date', *The Bar Review*, vol. 4, no. 5, 1999, p. 232.

constitutive of the public interest itself. The tribunal resides in the realm of objective fact; it is detached from social and subjective contexts. For the tribunal to embody the public interest, it would have to move beyond the limits of formal rationality and embrace what Habermas has termed 'normatively regulated action', that is, action directed at the normative expectations of the collectivity of Irish citizens. However reflexive the deliberations of a tribunal may be, the outcome invariably closes off the possibility of deliberative democracy. The work is completed, the report is written, and the roadshow (judges, lawyers, media and spectators) moves on. The very proliferation of tribunals means that they have become more and more formally ritualistic, repetitious and procedurally complex. Information has been collated, but there is no application of that knowledge in the democratic public sphere.

Representing the public interest: the role of the law and the media

The quest to identify and represent the public interest has resulted in considerable legal wrangling over the last few years. In the course of the Beef Tribunal, there was an expressed disagreement as to who represented the public interest – counsel for the tribunal or the Attorney General – since it was also the latter who represented the state authorities, thereby raising the spectre of a conflict of interest. Indeed, some lawyers have argued that 'what exactly the public interest was [in 1992] and how it should be represented, had become increasingly more difficult to define'.[12] Sara Moorhead goes on to argue that the old view that the Attorney General could represent the public interest, or the even older view that the tribunal itself could represent the public

---

12 S. Moorhead, 'Representing the public interest', Paper presented at the Bar Council of Ireland Seminar on Inquiries: The Rights of Individuals, Privacy and Confidentiality, 17 July 1999, p. 3.

interest, can no longer prevail, given the complexities of the public interest in the various state bodies requiring investigation. As a result, counsel for the public interest has been appointed in the Hepatitis C Tribunal and all subsequent tribunals.[13] But how can the public interest be defined? Through what mechanism can the public deliberate on the nature of their interest, and give expression to that interest?

The particular interest of the media, to have access to the information and to disseminate it, sometimes dovetails with the public interest, in the sense that the latter is also concerned with having access to all the information available. In this regard, the media may be seen as a watchdog for the public interest although it is not coterminous with the public interest. For example, it has been the media that has pushed the boundaries of what should constitute information 'in the public interest'. In the case of National Irish Bank (NIB), RTÉ sought the right to publish certain information it had received in relation to NIB account holders. The Supreme Court upheld the right of the media to publish, on the basis that the privacy rights of the account holder had to yield to the requirements of the public interest – in this case, the exposure of wrongdoing in a private financial institution.

The print and electronic media cover events as they unfold at the tribunal. The deliberations are enacted nightly on radio for those members of the public who cannot be present. Evidence is mediated into the public domain via the media. This reliance on the media once again renders the body politic as spectators, and not surprisingly, it is the more salacious aspects of the testimony and the antics of the principal characters that get most of the coverage.

---

13 In the case of the tribunal of inquiry on haemophiliacs and blood product contamination, constituted in 1999, the Attorney General has been charged with representing the public interest. So it appears that the matter of how the public interest should be represented and who should represent it is still open to contestation.

Irish democracy and the tribunals of inquiry

The former Chief Justice, Liam Hamilton, has said that if the proper questions had been asked and answered in the Dáil, it would have obviated the need for a Beef Tribunal in the early 1990s. The normal institutions of government, however, neither seem to be equipped nor motivated to solve the problems that have come to light in relation to the activities of various state agencies, politicians and businessmen. Admittedly, the politicians have begun to take on these issues, perhaps reflecting the impact of a nascent tribunal culture. In the autumn of 1999, the Dáil Public Accounts Committee (PAC) conducted a major televised investigation into the operation of the DIRT tax regime, with particular emphasis on the role of the banks. The PAC report was published in December 1999 and included sharp criticisms of both the banks and the state institutions. Added to this is the undoubted trust deficit which affects the public perception of politicians and ultimately their legitimacy in the eyes of the general public. This is most notable in the steadily declining participation by voters in elections. The ideological convergence of the main political parties may have also contributed to voters' apathy. In any event, politicians do not seem to be in a position to bring about disclosure.

According to Habermas, the unrest abroad in many established democracies 'has a deeper source, namely, the sense that in the age of a completely secularised politics, the rule of law cannot be had or maintained without radical democracy'.[14] But the tribunal, although it promises much, cannot be seen as an exercise in either deliberative or radical democracy. On the contrary, the tribunal more often resembles the kind of machinations we associate with pre-modern polities in its predilection for 'root[ing] out supposed wrongdoing and . . . the desire to reintroduce a modern-day version of the medieval village stock where supposed and

---

14 J. Habermas, *Between facts and norms: Contributions to a discourse theory of law and democracy*, Cambridge: Polity Press, 1996, p. xiii.

actual wrongdoers can be pelted with our collective venom and distaste through the mouths of Tribunal Counsel'.[15] What the public is party to in the era of the tribunal is the spectacularisation of democracy. At the tribunals, the democratic process is performed for public consumption, for media dissemination and for enactment. Its potential to carry the reflexive project into the public sphere is stymied by the limited statutory powers it is afforded.

The recent reliance on tribunals of inquiry does not herald the coming or strengthening of a deliberative democracy in Ireland. There is no reassurance that the core political institutions are now able to look at themselves critically and engage in appropriate reforms. The tribunals have been established in order to contain the widespread crisis of confidence in state institutions. In effect, they have had to manage a situation of crisis. Their role can be seen as that of closing an issue rather than opening it up for further consideration. Their task is to establish facts and not judge people – the proceedings in themselves cannot be used to pursue prosecutions. The tribunals have in a sense acted as deflectors of reflexivity. This tendency has been reinforced by the mass media, which has transformed the tribunals into spectacles and the public into spectators.

---

15 P. Gallagher, 'Tribunals and the erosion of the right to privacy', Paper presented at Bar Council of Ireland Seminar on Inquiries: The Rights of Individuals, Privacy and Confidentiality, 17 July 1999, p. 1.

EMBEDDED GLOBAL PROCESSES

CHAPTER 15

A Media Famine

EOIN DEVEREUX*

A great deal of what we know about what is happening elsewhere in the world is as a result of mass-mediatisation. The latter determines what people are informed about, how they are informed and indeed when they are informed. This chapter examines how a global issue is interpreted and dealt with at a local level: how a famine in Sudan is viewed from Ireland. It draws upon John Tomlinson's ideas about how one postcolonial society interprets another in a media setting.[1] Both Sudan and Ireland exhibit a high level of dependency on the global media industries; they rely on foreign news agencies in order to frame the 'story' of famine crises. Nevertheless, the local media appropriate these global issues through their own routines of news production.

The Sudanese crisis

The middle of 1998 witnessed the appeal of Irish aid agencies to the public for their help in assisting the people of southern

* The author would like to thank Amanda Haynes, University of Limerick, for her help.

1 J. Tomlinson, 'A phenomenology of globalisation? Giddens on global modernity', *European Journal of Communication*, vol. 9, 1994, pp. 149–172.

Sudan, who were once again facing the prospect of famine. It was variously estimated that between 350,000 and 700,000 people were at starvation point in the war zone in Bahr el Ghazal province.

The Irish print and broadcast media have been self-congratulatory in the past over their coverage of famine in places like Ethiopia and Rwanda. However, with the exception of *The Irish Times* and to a lesser extent RTÉ, they showed a marked reluctance to cover in any detailed way the threat or actuality of famine in southern Sudan. Public concern about the issue of African famine and poverty was demonstrated by the high levels of donations made to aid agencies such as Trócaire, Goal and Concern. Despite that, the interest of the Irish media in terms of either committing manpower or other resources to covering this Third World story remained low. Some journalists have pointed to the uncertainty of whether the Sudanese crisis constituted a famine or not. This argument highlights how Irish media coverage of Third World issues is generally crisis-driven and of a fire-brigade nature.

Media invisibility of the Third World

In Ireland, as in other modern societies, information is freely available to most at the click of a mouse; yet, there remains a deficit in the amount of debate and discussion about Third World issues. The lack of informed and critical analysis means that the Irish media conforms to patterns evident elsewhere in the developed world.

Sociologists, in attempting to explain the invisibility of Third World issues in a media context, have referred to the ethnocentrism of the media as well as its increasing emphasis on 'infotainment'. Even when it does manage to cover Third World crises, it often does so in the context of telling stories about the role of heroic (usually white) Western figures. The emphasis is usually placed on the short-term causes (such as climate, drought or crop failure) and the responses of Western governments and non-governmental organisations to the crisis in question. The primitivism of Africa, as well as an implicit suggestion of native culpability for crises of this kind, has also been commented upon. The over-concentration on the natural causes of food shortages and famine and on the responses of aid agencies to specific crises means that other more critical questions remain largely invisible. For instance, the exploitative relationship between the West and the Third World is largely unexplored. In short, the Western media tends to draw upon dominant ideological explanations for Third World crises.

In using the term ideology, I am following closely on the work of John B. Thompson, who in revising the term argued that ideology refers to 'meaning in the service of power'.[2] In the context of this chapter, we are interested in asking whether media coverage of Third World issues challenges or sustains the unequal relations of power which exist between the West and the Third World.

A cursory glance through the pages of the Irish print media in 1998 demonstrates that journalistic resources are taken up with an increasingly narrow range of domestic and foreign issues. The blurring of the traditional distinctions between 'information' and 'entertainment' has also resulted in a further reduction in 'hard news', whether from home or abroad. There is also some evidence to suggest that media professionals in Ireland and elsewhere have increasingly come to accept the view that audiences or readerships have grown jaded with the issue of African famine. In essence, African famine, which was once a big story, is no longer deemed to be newsworthy.

While increased media coverage, alleged charity fatigue and cultural and geographical distance may go some of the way towards explaining why the Third World remains relatively invisible in news terms, the way in which media organisations source stories and prioritise their journalistic activity is also significant. Organisational and editorial

---

2   J. B. Thompson, *Ideology and modern culture*, Cambridge: Polity Press, 1990.

decisions within a media organisation such as a newspaper or television station have a significant impact upon how social reality is ultimately constructed. Media organisations carve up their resources in a way that serves to prioritise certain kinds of stories over others. The commitment of a media organisation to covering the Third World can be measured in terms of its journalistic portfolio or at the very least by its willingness to send a journalist to report on Third World stories as they emerge. Even more tellingly in the Irish case, the print and broadcast media are heavily dependent on foreign news agencies for stories about the Third World. Media agendas are therefore set both within and outside of media organisations.

The Sudanese crisis presented an interesting challenge to the Irish media, not least because of the complexities involved in the civil war raging for fifteen years between the Muslim north and the Christian and animist south. In concurrence with Greg Philo's findings about the British media's reluctance to cover the 1984 Ethiopian famine, detailed and sustained media coverage of the Sudanese crisis was only to be found in the 'quality press', in this case *The Irish Times*.[3]

The Irish Times *and the Sudanese crisis*

We will now consider how *The Irish Times* covered the story of the Sudanese famine in 1998. We will examine the nature and extent of the coverage as well as considering the dominant discourses that were used to explain the reasons for the imminence of famine. While the dominant explanations given for the onset of famine – drought, crop failure, food shortages, civil war and local political corruption – conform to previous accounts of how the Western media explains African famine, there was also a significant amount of critical reflection in

---

3 G. Philo, 'From Buerk to Band-Aid: The Media and the 1984 Ethiopian Famine', in J. Eldridge (ed.), *Getting the message: News, truth and power*, London: Routledge, 1993.

the newspaper as to the reasons for and responses to the Sudanese crisis. A range of ideological positions is evident in the newspaper's coverage. While dominant ideological understandings of Third World famine can easily be identified in *The Irish Times* coverage, there is also in evidence a variety of explanations which either counter the accepted reasons for the Sudanese crisis or are at the very least critical in their orientation. This suggests that, while certain ideologies dominate, it is possible to find other ideological positions within more critical forms of media coverage.

The Irish Times is the only mainstream newspaper in the Republic of Ireland with a journalist dedicated to covering development issues. In the past it had the post of 'Africa correspondent' amongst its journalistic portfolios. More recently it has published special supplements which deal with the developing world. In late 1996, it appointed its first development correspondent, whose brief is to cover development issues in both Ireland and the developing world. The correspondent has a specific responsibility to cover stories in developing countries as they arise.

Between April and August 1998, *The Irish Times* published a total of twenty-two stories about the famine crisis in the Bahr el Ghazal province of southern Sudan. Beginning with coverage in April, the telling of the story peaked in the months of May and June with a reduced amount of coverage in July and August. The initial coverage came from foreign news agency sources, and while the majority of stories were written by the paper's development correspondent, a small number of stories and opinion pieces were written by other staff journalists, freelance journalists, development workers, aid agency representatives and an Irish government minister. The wide-ranging nature of the coverage in terms of themes ensured to a certain extent the longevity of the story.

The cycle of the story

The cycle of the Sudanese story in *The Irish Times* began on 6 April 1998 with the initial warnings from aid agencies about the need for assistance in the form of food, seeds and tools. From the beginning it was stated that the Sudanese crisis could only be resolved through a combination of humanitarian aid and the political pressure needed to resolve the civil war. By 18 April the newspaper warned that people were beginning to die from famine in southern Sudan; 350,000 people were said to be at risk. The report noted the logistical problems caused by the refusal of the Khartoum government to give permission for humanitarian flights to drop food and supplies in southern Sudan. The civil war was cited as the key reason for the onset of famine.

Bob Geldof's appearance on the BBC's *Six O'Clock News* served to guarantee further coverage of the Sudanese crisis by the print media. The follow-up report in *The Irish Times* (25 April 1998) conformed to the argument that much of what we learn about the Third World is in terms of the activities or utterances of elite, white, Western figures. The fact that a heroic (and Irish) figure had made a statement about the potential crisis in Sudan increased the possibility that the BBC story would be picked up by the Irish print media. As a piece of journalism, it is illustrative of the dependency of the Irish media on others in reporting on the Third World. The story is of interest in that it draws upon both the BBC report of the previous evening and also uses additional material from the Guardian Service news agency.

The month of May witnessed a number of shifts in terms of how the story was being told to *The Irish Times*' readership. On 4 May, the original estimation of those at risk from famine was doubled to 700,000. The international pressure being brought to bear on both sides of the conflict resulted in a resumption of peace talks, although the logistical problems in delivering aid continued. *The Irish Times* then began to concentrate on reporting on Irish aid efforts – how the Irish government and aid agencies were responding to the crisis.

The coverage of the crisis then switched to a more critical discourse as the Khartoum government began to allow a limited amount of flights into southern Sudan. *The Irish Times* now began to concentrate on how the Khartoum government was attempting to use hunger as a weapon in the civil war. The newspaper also reflected upon the dilemmas facing aid agencies.

The aid agencies realised that the timing of their appeals to their respective publics via the media in the West had to be strategic. If they raised money and the Khartoum government continued to restrict or refuse flights of mercy to the region, then there was the possibility that the public might lose interest or stop donating. It was also noted that many observers now believed that the public was suffering from charity fatigue. The collection and distribution of aid was not therefore determined by the immediate needs of the famine victims in southern Sudan, but rather by the way in which media coverage could be best managed. The response of the public in Ireland and elsewhere was determined by the flow of media coverage – not by real time, but by media time – within the global media industries. The aid agencies faced the prospect, in their need to deliver humanitarian aid, of having to choose between one or other side in the civil war.

The newspaper's development correspondent went to Sudan in late May. The immediate result of this was an obvious increase in the extent of detailed reporting and analysis. His reports described the conditions facing the southern Sudanese and attempted to assess whether they constituted a famine or a threat of famine. The coverage extended to examining the underlying reasons for the crises in Africa and made specific reference to colonialism.[4] Some of the themes from the earlier coverage – the heroic Irish aid worker, the manipulation and misuse of humanitarian aid by the Khartoum government, repeated warnings about the imminence of famine – were central to how the story was told in the month of June.

The coverage took on an even more critical tone on 6 June when the paper considered the role of the Western media in

4 P. Cullen, 'Sudan straddles religious and political faultline', *The Irish Times,* 30 May 1998.

reporting (or failing to report) on African issues. *The Irish Times* noted that some of the Western media's representatives had filmed polio-stricken children as famine victims. In 'Media do Africa few favours in rush to meet deadlines', Paul Cullen argued that a key theme in recent media coverage of African crises was that:

> The aid agencies failed to alert the world to the disaster . . . until the media rode in to the rescue. A pity then that the image is misleading. Visit any village in Africa and you will find children with polio. The reasons for this have nothing to do with hunger in Southern Sudan. They have everything to do with shrinking aid budgets, local mismanagement and the crippling debt burden Western banks impose on poor countries. But you won't find these topics often on the diet of primetime television news. The girl in the camera lens is likely to go on suffering long after Sudan becomes a fading line in the reporter's curriculum vitae.

The response of the EU and the necessity of a political solution in order to end the immediate crisis in Sudan were equally persistent themes.

The Irish Times carried an article on 4 July which attempted to counter the views previously expressed in the newspaper as to the actual causes of the famine crisis.[5] The coverage ended in August with reports on the visit of an Irish government minister to Sudan as well as a critical 'World-View' opinion piece by the chief executive of an Irish Third World agency.

For *The Irish Times* and other media organisations, the newsworthiness of the story ended when international humanitarian aid began to get through to the Sudanese and famine was averted. The problems inherent in alerting the public to the crisis without the political dimension being

---

5 Y. Al-Hussein, 'Stop the war and the famine will end', *The Irish Times*, 4 July 1998.

resolved meant that many journalists felt there was nothing more to add to the famine story. It had lost its newsworthiness.

The Irish Times provided detailed and analytical coverage of the issue. Its commitment to covering such issues was evident at an editorial and at a resource level. In terms of ideological content, *The Irish Times* coverage conforms to most of the patterns previously identified by John Horgan in his analysis of the 1984 African famine.[6] There was, however, a significant amount of critical coverage of the causes of, and responses to, African crises in the newspaper; a limited amount of coverage countered the 'accepted' understanding of the crisis. Unlike media coverage of previous famine crises, in Ethiopia for example, there was no reference to Ireland's 'famine-memory' as being the underlying reason for the scale of the public response to the famine crisis.

The local and the global

Tomlinson has placed a particular emphasis on the question of the mediation of experience. While globalisation stretches the relations between the distant and the local, he argues that the concept of mediation implies that experience passes through an 'intermediary'.[7] He is referring here to the role of the mass media in linking distant events with the everyday experience of those living in late modernity and is questioning the true extent to which the world has become more 'open'.

The mass media are clearly responsible for the increased volume of information which social actors are now offered. We are not however living in a 'global village' where information and knowledge flow freely between continents. The global media industry has immense power in terms of how it

---

6 J. Horgan, 'Africa and Ireland: Aspects of a media agenda', *Trócaire Development Review*, 1987.

7 J. Tomlinson, 'A phenomenology of globalisation? Giddens on global modernity', *European Journal of Communication*, vol. 9, 1994, p. 155.

covers events outside of the developed world. Global news agencies and major broadcasting organisations are primarily responsible for the selection and packaging of news from the Third World. Third World countries have an obvious dependency on the global media industry, and especially so in times of crisis when news has to travel fast. In this light, the media coverage of Third World issues sustains the unequal relations of power that exist between the West and the Third World. Yet, despite the growing dominance of the West through media globalisation, the local does not play its part in how particular stories are received.

Global issues such as famine or poverty, although experienced through the mass media, are nonetheless appropriated through a local prism. Media audiences are exposed to stories about faraway places and events, but these stories place a heavy emphasis on local involvement. Thus, many of the stories about the Sudanese crisis focused on the Irish response, both voluntary and statutory, and celebrated the heroic role of the Irish aid worker. The process of globalisation now at work links, in a rather direct way, locales to large structures and occurrences. But the reverse also holds true: local factors play a strong role in the way global processes are experienced. The latter have to make themselves local in order to become effective.

CHAPTER 16

The Archaeology of Irish Golfscapes

EAMONN SLATER

If you want inner peace, find it in solitude, not speed. And if you would find yourself, look to the land from which you came and to which you go (Henry David Thoreau).

The majority of us are living in urban areas and it is difficult for us to connect to the 'land'. Access and opportunity are extremely limited. However, one means of finding 'inner peace' in the land continues to exist and that is golf. Golf has become extremely popular in Ireland. In April 1998, the Minister for Tourism, Sport and Recreation, Dr James McDaid TD, announced that Ireland had become the 'Mecca for golf in Europe':

> It was not by accident that we succeeded in securing the staging of the Ryder Cup in 2005. With our growing reputation in the world of golf and the excellent courses and facilities available here we were bound to be a strong contender.[1]

Dr McDaid then went on to reveal that Irish golf was now being broadcast on American television:

---

1 'How we are taking Irish golf to the world', *Irish Golf Monthly*, April 1998, p. 2.

While the Ryder Cup may seem some time away, I can assure you that Ireland is already gaining much attention on the golfing channels in the United States.

From this viewpoint, it could be argued that golf in Ireland has come of age. Golf is now an activity that can be transmitted to the world through modern technology. Its presence as a global entity is becoming recognised. Scooping the Ryder Cup can be seen as indicative of this trend. There has been much discussion, and a lot of it heated, as to why the Ryder Cup will be coming not just to Ireland but to the K Club in County Kildare. Much of the debate is concerned with a conflict between the traditional members-run clubs and the new privately owned clubs. The issue essentially revolves around money and the cost of holding the event. However, one aspect of the difference between these two contesting types of club that fails to get mentioned, is that they also represent two differing types of course design. One native, which has emerged from the old parkland estates, the other the new 'American type' course. With the appearance of the latter into Ireland, we have an example of how a global entity has become 'localised'. Within the global arena, according to Robins, economies and cultures are thrown into intense and immediate contact with each other – with each 'other' (an 'other' that is no longer simply 'out there' but also within).[2] In this chapter, I will examine how the presence of the 'American type' golf course is impacting on the local courses. The overall conclusion to be reached is that local courses are not only being globalised through design but also through increased capital costs and increased costs of access. In these ways local space is being globalised.

Golf has been widely played in Ireland for over a hundred years. Recently, however, there has been a major upsurge in the number of people playing the game – the number actually doubled between 1974 and 1994. According to Arnold Horner,

2 K. Robins, 'Global times', *Marxism Today*, December 1989.

the supply of golf facilities has also increased to meet this demand. Between 1990 and 1994, 73 new courses were built, another 44 were extended (from nine to eighteen holes) and 35 more were being planned. During the 1990s Ireland's golf capacity expanded by over 50 per cent. The greatest 'boom' has been around Dublin, where there will be over 90 courses available within a forty-mile radius of the city centre by 1999.

The reason for this massive growth, according to Horner, is that the essential structure of the game has moved from being a player-driven sport to being a major investment for business entrepreneurs in the post-industrial world. Like all business ventures, these new enterprises need to attract customers. One essential aspect of attracting attention and hopefully customers is to make the golf course an exciting spectacle. To achieve this status it has to be packaged and sold through the visual media: the golf magazines, the Internet and especially television broadcasting. Therefore the game of golf, both locally and globally, has become a visual commodity in the global media industries. In doing so, the backdrop to this sporting activity has been transformed in order to heighten the pleasure from viewing golf. This strategy has worked, not only locally but also globally. In terms of space, Irish golf courses have expanded greatly. According to Horner:

> The creation of a golf course represents a major land-scape development. Its scale and impact in rural areas is at present only paralleled by some major quarry developments and by afforestation projects. Visually it can be seen as a twentieth century parallel to the eighteenth century demesne . . .[3]

However, the dramatic link between the modern golf courses and the eighteenth-century demesnes may not be just about

---

3 A. Horner, 'Golf course development: Dilemmas of activity tourism', in P. Breathnach (ed.), *Irish Tourism Development*, Maynooth: Geographical Society of Ireland, 1994, p. 87.

spatial expansion but also may involve a similar appreciation of the landscape aesthetic.

Prehistory of the local golfscape

The emergence of the English-style garden of the eighteenth century into the Irish landed estates was revolutionary. As a design, it demanded that flowers, fruit and vegetables be banished to walled gardens, away from the house; and that formal features, such as parterres, avenues and canals, be swept away and replaced with an idealised conception of 'natural' landscapes. The greatest exponent of this informal style was Capability Brown. Brown applied the compositional principles of landscape painting and worked them through three basic mediums of wood, water and grass. Although, in spatial terms, the Brownian landscape was dominated by grass and water (lakes), it was the tree that created the dramatic effect in this 'natural' garden. Grass and water tend to be monotonous in tone and lacking in visual variety. In contrast, the tree, because of its physical variety and its differing colour tones, became the actual 'brush strokes' of the landscape gardener. By mixing broadleaf with evergreen trees and by placing them along differing planes in the landscape, the landscape gardener was able to achieve the same effect as the painters did in perspective. But crucially, this reproduction was not a mere representation of landscape, it was the real thing – a real landscape designed to look picturesque.

Accordingly, the picturesque landscape within the estate was designed to impress the mind of the viewer. In the consumption of the picturesque views, a state of harmony was sought between the individual and the 'natural' surrounds – an Arcadia without disharmony. Unsightly objects and ugly images were hidden from view. Since this estate landscape was theme-parked into a leisure garden, one of the essential principles of the project was to eliminate the appearance of work from the horizon. A number of strategies were developed to achieve this disappearing trick. Tree clumps were planted in order to screen off the productive area of the estate. Some estates had service tunnels and sunken roads dug so that the supply of goods and services to the 'Big House' might take place without disturbing the peace and tranquillity of the park. Even the estate walls were hidden from view behind a curtain of trees and scrubs.

Therefore, these theme-parked gardens were constructed in such a way as to convey a sense of freedom. Freedom with regard to a person's ability to move through the landscape without being apparently impeded by a fence or a stone wall. And because of the existence of the estate walls, the parkland connoisseurs could roam freely without the possibility of running into 'undesirables'. These illusionary constructs were an attempt to create an Arcadian world without constraints. And because of the essential relationship of spectators and the land, the actual landscape was changed to suit the wishes of the landscape connoisseurs.

As a consequence, the eighteenth-century aesthetic of the picturesque dramatically transformed particular areas of the Irish landscape. According to Terrence Reeves-Smyth, by the middle of the nineteenth century, parkland occupied around 800,000 acres or 4 per cent of Ireland, with over 7,000 houses featuring pleasure landscapes of ten acres or more.[4] But these old picturesque landscapes are not entirely lost in the past, for some of them are being rejuvenated as the physical backdrop to the game of golf. Let us attempt to discover how the Brownian framework has penetrated into Irish golfscapes.

Local Brownian golfscapes

To do this I want to look at a typical course in Ireland, one, which has not been 'Americanised'. The first scene is of a fairway.

---

4 T. Reeves-Smyth, 'Demesnes', in F. H. A. Aalen, K. Whelan and M. Stout (eds.), *Atlas of the Irish landscape*, Cork: Cork University Press, 1997, p. 20.

It is not obvious that this is a scene from a golf course – but it is. The physical manifestation of golf activity on the terrain is extremely limited except for the possibility of a raised green and the flagpole on the horizon. What is significant is that the surrounding landscape is typically Brownian in structure. The rolling grassland seems to stretch to the horizon, which is framed on both sides by clumps of trees. There is no evidence of work being carried out. It all looks like it has been left to nature. There does not seem to be any order imposed on the landscape. For example, there are no boundaries visible. All of these characteristics help to maintain that essential sense of freedom – freedom of movement – that is crucial in the ideological construction of Arcadia. And finally there is no evidence of other people present in the landscape or of their constructs on the landscape. In typically Brownian fashion, it all looks so natural – as every picturesque garden should.

In the second picture of this golf course, we have a view of a green surrounded by sand bunkers. I will draw

attention to the shape of these bunkers in order to illustrate how a non-Brownian feature can become Brownian in its composition and form. According to Lamb and Bowe, the modelling of the ground into artistic swellings and curves was an effect much prized by the Brownian school in Ireland.[5] Such a 'swelling' can be seen on the sides of these bunkers as they curve into the grassland. Even a trap gets the Brownian treatment. There are no apparent artificial straight edges in this landscape to indicate the impact of society on it. Nature, as in the picturesque parklands of old, seems to be reigning supreme.

Finally, we have a more panoramic view of this fairway. This is a beautiful representation of the Brownian aesthetic. The golf course and how it has been represented here exudes all the features of the picturesque landscape. This process of

5 K. Lamb and P. Bowe, *A history of gardening in Ireland*, Dublin: National Botanic Gardens, 1995.

aestheticisation is further heightened by the presence of snow in the photograph. But although the aesthetic of the course is essentially Brownian, there are features that have been changed in order to accommodate the actual playing of golf. In spatial terms, the amount of trees has been lessened in order to create a playing passage from the tee box to the green. As a consequence, the amount of area given over to grass has increased proportionately. But, crucially, like the original Brownian landscape of old, the aesthetic of this terrain was to be appreciated by moving through it. It is a player's view. Therefore, the physical design of the old picturesque courses confirms the point that Horner made, namely that the structure of the pre-Americanised game was essentially 'a player-driven sport'.

The iron cage within the golfscape

We have already identified how the picturesque framework was constructed as an escape from the constraints of modern industrial and urban life. In a sense, it was an attempted pilgrimage into the spirituality of nature for the newly emerged upper middle classes. The reconstructed informal garden of the picturesque provided the ideal haven for these exhausted captains of industry and not a straight line or right angle to remind them of the precision of performance required from them in their everyday work routines. But the contemporary pilgrims from modernity do bring an iron cage of calculability with them as they tee off in these modern picturesque parklands and that is the grid of laws and regulations of golf which guide a golfer through the landscape. These abstract constructs determine not only how one relates to the landscape but also establish how one moves through the terrain. Under these conditions of constraint, there is no hope of discovering one's true self. In short, it is impossible to appreciate the scenic qualities of a particular fairway when one is putting for an eagle. In a sense, the golfing experience detaches one from accessing 'nature' through the framework of the picturesque. As a consequence, what the picturesque backdrop to the golf experience does is to merely lure the golfer away from his or her routine through its media representation without any hope of overcoming his or her alienation in the first place. There does not seem to be any way out of the tightening cages of modernity – certainly not on the picturesque golf courses of Ireland. But these Irish picturesque courses are themselves being transformed by a new aesthetic – a global one.

The global television aesthetic

In late modernity, with increased televising of golf and the restructuring of the Irish golfing landscape, we get the emergence of Ireland's new spectacular golf courses – the K Club, Mount Juliet, Druid's Glen and Portmarnock Links – which have been specifically designed to hold major European Tour events. I use the word 'spectacular' in two senses. Firstly, as a television spectacle and secondly, to allow a large amount of spectators to see the event live. In Ireland, the consequence of this visualisation process within the sport of golf is that courses have been designed to appeal essentially to a television audience. This new style is generally known as the American style; where sand bunkers and water hazards have been spectacularly expanded in spatial terms. But crucially, these new courses demand a huge capital investment – and this investment requires adequate financial return. In consequence, they need to lure money to themselves, either from high-fee-paying members or green fee players – the golfing tourists, or preferably both. These golfing tourists can be either foreign or local. In fact the most lucrative niche of this market is the local society outings and corporate 'days', where the entire day is booked by one business institution for its employees and customers. What is crucial to this particular tourist market is that the courses need to lure these golfing tourists onto them by emphasising their exotic aspects. Horner highlights one of the essential exotic features of Irish golf courses for the foreign golfer:

> The attraction of playing unhustled golf in scenic, naturally green surroundings, whether on seaside links or in parkland settings, are considerable for many Europeans. Space, scenery, emptiness and the opportunity to play at will for moderate green fees are qualities that can be at premium in city-region Europe yet they are potentially readily available on an Irish golfing holiday.[6]

In this quotation Irish golf courses are being conceptualised as a means of escape – escape from not only urban Europe into the Irish rural countryside, but also from the congestion that can exist on European courses onto the emptiness of under-utilised Irish courses. But crucially, Irish golf is being

---

6 A. Horner, 'Golf course development: Dilemmas of activity tourism', in P. Breathnach (ed.), *Irish Tourism Development*, Maynooth: Geographical Society of Ireland, 1994, p. 89.

seen as a departure from the normal practices of playing golf on the continent. Therefore, the essential determinant of the recent restructuring of Irish golf is that it should become a successful tourist product. The interesting aspect of this development is that the vast majority of these new courses have been constructed on old estate parklands. For example, of the four 'spectacular' courses mentioned above, three were developed from old parklands.

However, these 'spectacular' courses have been redesigned in light of their visual appeal to the TV cameras. Specifically, how they are able to pan over the terrain from an aerial elevation. This is achieved by using helicopters and high camera locations from extended crane elevations. Therefore, the most common images of golf and its backdrop circulating in the global media are ones from the 'bird's eye' perspective. Accordingly, the picturesque aesthetic of the old parkland courses has been transformed into the television aesthetic. This new aesthetic has expanded the space occupied by sand bunkers and water hazards in order to appeal to the armchair viewers of the sport rather than to the actual players of the game.

Local golf on more globalised golfscapes

The emergence of the television aesthetic in the Irish golfscape has had a number of important consequences for the structure of Irish golf. The penetration of the television aesthetic has occurred unevenly. The new 'spectacular' courses are extremely expensive to construct and maintain. Large amounts of capital are required to produce such a product. Local members' clubs are not able to accumulate this scale of funding. Only private enterprises can run these entities, not only as a local attraction but also as a potential location for a global event like the Ryder Cup. But the local courses cannot isolate themselves completely from these 'spectacular' global entities standing in their midst. Because the market for Irish golf is being dictated by the big 'spectacular' clubs, their design features are beginning to influence the type of physical reconstructing of the local courses. More and more of the Americanised aesthetic features are being incorporated into the old picturesque golf courses as they attempt to keep up with these global trend-setters, for example more water and sand hazards. But there is a price to be paid for such a slavish following of fashion, the cost of entry for members and for the golfing tourist has to be increased in order to meet the increased costs of the reconstruction. Also, more time may have to be allotted to those golfers who can provide the greatest financial return in the short term – the golfing tourist. The impact of all of these trends on the ordinary playing member is that access to one's own course will become more and more restricted in order to meet these new financial demands. Here we have an example of another iron cage of modernity being spun around the potential escapee from late modernity. And this new cage is being determined by complex global forces, which are not easily discernible on the 'ground' of these new golfscapes of Ireland. An archaeological dig was necessary to uncover these abstract forces of globalisation and how they are impacting on the local golf courses of Ireland.

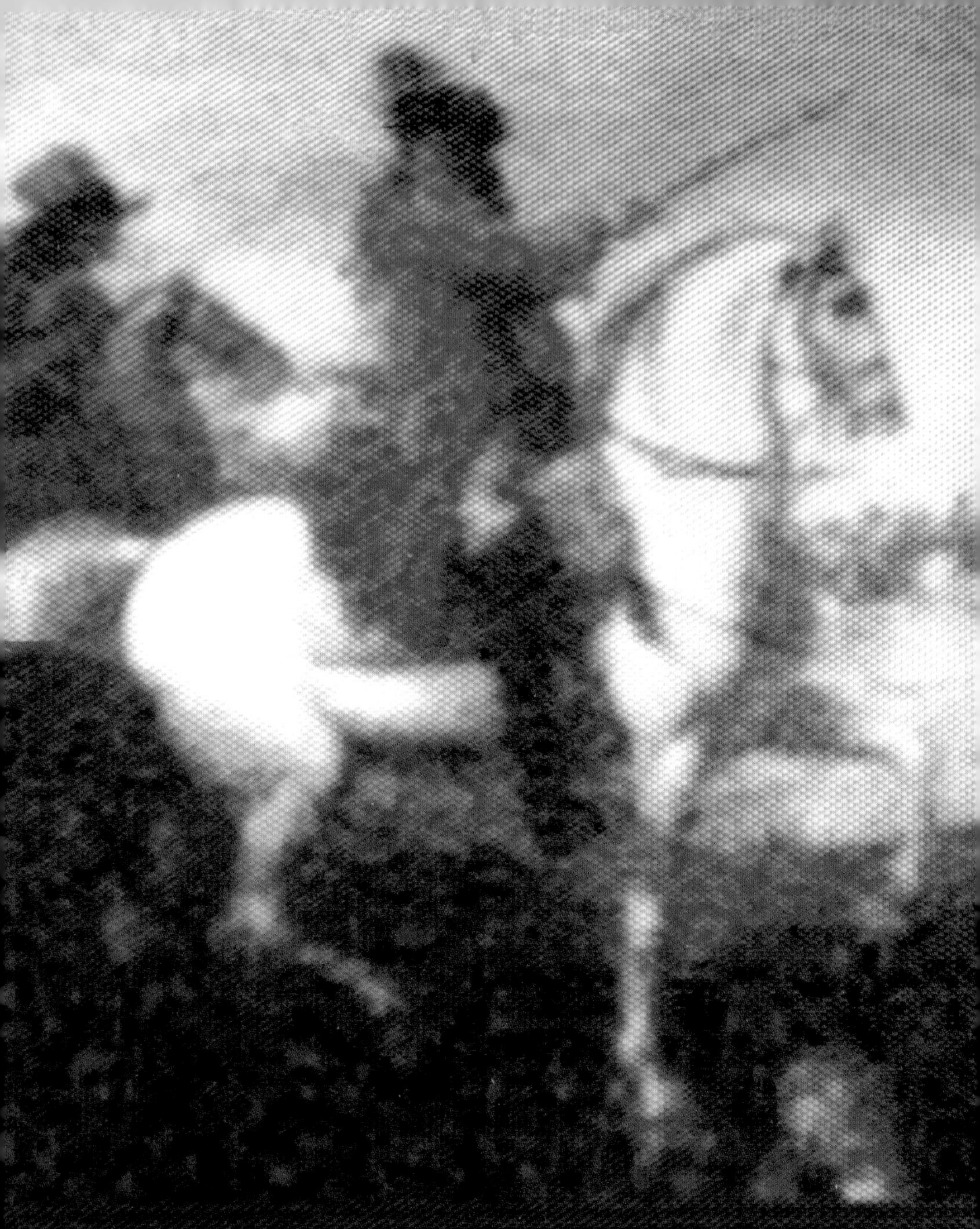

orangelink

Dividing Loyalties: Local Identities in a Global Economy

JIM SMYTH AND DAVID CAIRNS

The verbal encounter between the nationalist Molly Ivors and 'West Briton' Gabriel Conroy is one of the most vivid scenes in Joyce's *Dubliners'* story 'The Dead'. Gabriel's sin, in Molly's eyes, lies in his refusal to go on a month's retreat to the Aran Islands, in favour of a cycling trip 'to France or Belgium or perhaps Germany', thereby rejecting his Irish identity.[1] The memorability of the episode lies in the fact that today in Ireland few would see the western seaboard as a repository of the core values of their Irishness and even fewer would resent Gabriel's cosmopolitanism. Gabriel himself might now be willing to visit the west, safe in the belief that he would be comfortable in one of the many enclaves carved out by the would-be cosmopolitans of Dublin 4.

The fracturing of the classic dichotomised Irish national identity is aptly encapsulated in the now redundant phrase 'West Briton'. Today, the dominant groups in the Republic embrace cosmopolitanism as a virtue and shun nationalism

---

1 "O, to tell you the truth," retorted Gabriel suddenly, "I'm sick of my own country, sick of it!", J. Joyce, 'Dubliners', in H. Levin (ed.), *The essential James Joyce*, Harmondsworth: Penguin, 1967.

as an embarrassing relic. The break with nationalist discourse has been swift and virtually uncontested, but the 'spiritual liberation' which Joyce hoped would replace the stifling confines of Catholic nationalism has proved elusive. The undeniable material liberation, at least for a significant section of the population, from the constraints of a paralysed, comatose, clientelist economy has opened up a moral and political vacuum. It has exposed the corrupt heart of the once unassailable institutions of the nationalist state. One important effect of these changes has been to fracture the organic and emotional links to nationalists in the north, where the same forces which have so dramatically transformed the south have broken and fragmented on the reefs of a divided society.

Globalisation and the erosion of the nation-state

The forces that have transformed the Republic's economy and society have been largely external and global. Globalisation dissolves the traditional boundaries and internal structures of nation-states and communities, as change expresses itself in the ever-increasing mobility of capital, information, commodities and people across what were once impermeable borders and frontiers. Hence, the weakening of the institutions of the nation-state and its traditional economic protectionist policies is an essential part of this process. With economic globalisation comes cultural change, as the increased mobility of capital, labour and information dissolves traditional classes, communities and groups, and introduces a global culture.

Globalisation is also an inherently uneven process. Its effect depends on the ability and willingness of indigenous cultural forms to resist or embrace globalisation. Given Ireland's history of economic and social failure since independence,[2] it was no surprise to find globalisation greeted as a

---

2 J. Lee, *Ireland 1922–1985,* Cambridge: Cambridge University Press, 1989.

panacea. The baggage of national independence was cast aside with almost indecent haste. Nowhere else in Europe was there, for instance, less debate about the wisdom of joining the European single currency. Therefore, the Irish political, media and business elite swiftly endorsed the erosion of national independence and, watched by a cynical electorate, embraced a new subservient status within the EU.

The paradox of globalisation is that while it weakens the cohesion of traditional nation-states, it can also motivate minorities to seek identity in sub-national groups and the politics of the local, chiefly when such minorities are disenfranchised. The cultural forms typical of globalisation depend on the media for their transmission and influence: a culture, profoundly anti-historical, which devalues the past as a narrative and the source for an imagined community within which people can locate themselves and their others. The rejection of history and progress is central to such a culture, which replaces continuity with simulacra: images or representations of the past which permit no sense of the past. However, Smith argues that the very 'nature' of such a culture may preclude the possibility of creating an alternative identity focused on the global rather than on the national or local, as:

> ... images and traditions can be sustained only if they have some popular resonance, and will have this resonance only if they can be harmonised and made continuous with a perceived collective past ... a memoryless culture is a contradiction: any attempt to create such a global culture would simply accentuate the plurality of folk memories and identities that have been plundered in order to constitute this giant bricolage.[3]

---

3 A. D. Smith, *National identity,* London: Penguin, 1981. See also J. Smyth, 'Nacionalismo, globalizatcion y movimientos sociales', in P. Ibarra and B. Tejerina (eds.), *Los movimentos sociales: Transformaciones politicas y cambio cultural,* Madrid: Trotta, 1998.

The state in the Republic has been effectively superseded by a plethora of overarching transnational relations, over which the hollowed-out institutions of state power have little control. The privileged citizens, those who have knowledge of the system's workings, are already detached from their national culture of origin. The implosion of the traditional institutions of Irish independence: the Catholic Church, the political class and now the judiciary, has dismantled potential institutional bulwarks capable of reacting against encroaching globalisation and granted free passage to the ideologues of transnational capital. With the dissolution of the traditional bonds of community and class, divisions in Ireland rest less upon exploitation than exclusion. For instance, while the country has the highest rate of economic growth in Europe, one-third of its population is at risk of poverty and almost 15 per cent live in a persistent state of poverty.

One crucial difference between the Republic and Northern Ireland is the way in which the effects of this change are debated. In the south, there has been a virtual absence of either national or local resistance and an almost total lack of public debate about the type of society that might emerge from increasing global integration; issues such as marginalisation, exclusion, and institutional reform thus remain at the margins of debate. Meanwhile, in the north, such problems take centre stage.

Identity, culture and conflict in a divided society

In the divided society of the north, socio-economic cleavages have typically coalesced around sectarianised principles of ethnicity, religion, territory and culture, which have also become pivotal to the process of 'defining' identity. Until 1968, the unionist-dominated Stormont state successfully repressed any tendency towards the assertion of ethno-national aspirations on the part of the Catholic and nationalist minority. Monolithic political unionism and the populist culture of Orangeism welded together various Protestant groupings under the principle of loyalty to the

British crown, believing that Britain would constitutionally protect their way of life. The official discourse of this 'unified' unionism incorporated notions of modernisation, democracy and loyalty, whilst simultaneously disregarding the political and cultural aspirations of the minority Catholic population. The homogenous character of Irish nationalism (where the main internal cleavage remains over means, not ends) made this repression and exclusion a relatively simple operation.

Unlike the relationship between Catholicism and nationalism, interrelations within Protestantism are more complex. Groupings within Protestantism range from fundamentalist/ evangelical schisms (the number of people in this category is put at a not insignificant 100,000) who derive their politics from theology, to 'moderate unionists' who espouse an interpretation of modernisation and secularisation which traditionally branded the Republic as socially, economically and politically backward. Between these two poles are the constantly interweaving and mutating groupings which stress the regional identity of Ulster, others who emphasise the Scottish or English legacy, and further groups who postulate a particular brand of Irishness. Since the onset of the current unrest and armed conflict after 1968, the ability of the unionist parties to politically harmonise these disparate strands has been shattered. Three principal reasons account for this: the reluctance of some mainstream unionists to compromise with nationalist demands through participation in the Good Friday Agreement, the gradual withdrawal of the British state from its traditional unionist position and the effects of globalisation.

This fracture translates into a reality where a considerable minority of Protestants feel increasingly marginalised both within their 'own' community and in terms of their wider socio-economic position. They are unable to resist 'outside' attempts at curtailing their exclusively loyalist marching practices of Orangeism.[4] The excluded, impotent and

---

4 The following three quotes are taken from D. Cairns, *Sectarianism in popular culture,* unpublished DPhil thesis, Coleraine: University of Ulster, 1999.

demonised character of loyalism is ably expressed in this quotation, taken from an interview with a loyalist woman:

> All this old nonsense . . . say for example the issue about parades. Ten years ago, you know, you had your twelfth of July and there's nothing said about it. The Catholics just didn't mind, but me, I believe there's an element in the Catholics just doing it, stirring things up, just for badness so, you know, we look to be the 'bad boys' [with] their 'triumphal marches down our roads' an' all. Before they would never've cared. You walked on and you would've got to your church and had your Sunday service and they would've even come out to see you. But now they're all into 'mind twisting' and making us all out to be real bigots. And it's just not right. Tryin' to take away our freedom, and it is definitely part of our culture. It's politically incorrect to fly the Union Jack. It's politically incorrect or inappropriate to sing the Queen. It's politically incorrect to say you are British.

It is 'local' feelings of disrespect such as these that provide the dynamic impetus for contestations such as the annual Drumcree 'stand-off' and the romanticisation of Orangeism as the upholder of Protestant freedom in the face of threats from Westminster, Dublin and beyond. It is therefore no accident that the locus of Protestant dissatisfaction is located in areas where unemployment and social deprivation coincide with traditional fundamentalism and Orangeism, for example Portadown/Lurgan and Antrim/Ballymena. The fracturing of unionism has had the effect of shifting the locus of conflict, from the political to the cultural arena, for a significant and militant minority section of the Protestant population centred in these enclaves. Shifts of this nature are a common feature of contemporary complex societies, as the politics of identity becomes a motive force of local resistance to globalisation.

Identity politics have a fundamentally reactive and defensive form, focused upon the defence of a politicised culture in the face of political uncertainty and rapid socio-economic change. It is not surprising that the Orange Order, the most prominent transmission vehicle of Protestant resistance to political and social change, along with its cognate organisations (the Apprentice Boys of Derry and the Royal Black Preceptory), has become a means of popular protest. The Orange Order and its annual series of ritual marches provides a ready-made platform; its decentralised structure also makes it susceptible to grass-roots demands.

For many Protestants, and not only those who are members, the Orange Order embodies a crucial element of their identity: a shared ethnic history of an imagined community heroically depicted as continual resistors to change and what they see as oppression from the Catholic Church, the Dublin government and the nationalist community. Through its rituals, individual and family histories are integrated with this broader Protestant discourse, as the following quotations from two Orangemen illustrate:

> There is that aspect of it, where there is a great family tradition . . . my father, all my uncles, my grandfather, my great grandfather and so on, right back literally as far as the formation of the Orange Order itself, were all the members of the lodge that I'm in, that hopefully my young lad will join. His choice, but hopefully he will.

The second respondent, a county grand master of the Order, also links family tradition with broader historical processes:

> Again it's tradition . . . My father was a member of the Orange Order and from an early age, they carried me as a child [to marches]. [It's a] family tradition. It was just passed on to me, from my father, and I got involved and I still have an interest in it as I say. [Now] I'm County Master, in charge of a whole county. But again tradition is there.

This deeply emotive, almost primordial, identification between certain marginalised Protestants and the Orange institution has intensified as the link between the Ulster

Unionist Party and the Order in the post-Stormont period has weakened. The sense of betrayal and exclusion felt by many Protestants forces them back onto more basic expressions of identity, what Manuel Castells terms 'cultural communes', characterised by three main features:

> They appear as reactions to prevailing social trends, which are resisted on behalf of autonomous sources of meaning. They are, at their onset, defensive identities that function as refuge and solidarity, to protect against a hostile, outside world. They are culturally constituted; that is, organised around a specific set of values whose meaning and sharing are marked by specific codes of self identification: the community of believers, the icons of nationalism, the geography of locality.[5]

Seen in a broader context, reinvigorated identification with the Orange Order is an example of how a section of a community, disenchanted with the failure of the nation-state to deal with exclusion and marginalisation, channels its resistance through established organisations, albeit with a new vocabulary and a discursive strategy of stressing its cultural and political disempowerment. But what has changed in the relationship is the position of the Order within the state: the Protestant 'right' to march is no longer officially legitimised. Today, the Order is forced to justify its marching practices through making recourse to cultural, traditional and civil libertarian argumentation frames. As the Grand Orange Lodge of Ireland illustrates:

> Parades are very much part of the Orange tradition and heritage as two hundred years ago the founding fathers decided that parades were the appropriate

---

5 M. Castells, *The rise of the network society*, Volume 1, Oxford: Blackwell, 1996, p. 65. See also A. Touraine, *A critique of modernity*, Oxford: Blackwell, 1996; and A. Melucci, *Challenging codes. Collective action in the Information Age*, Cambridge: Cambridge University Press, 1996.

medium to witness for their faith and to celebrate their cultural heritage.[6]

Conclusion

Both parts of Ireland have been subject to broadly similar structural changes during the last three decades of the twentieth century: the collapse of traditional industry, significant shifts in the class structure and a decline in the power of the state. Neither region has been immune to the effects of globalisation upon culture and identity, although responses have significantly differed. In the south, the manifest failure of independence to free the country from its economic and social ills fostered the decline of organisations such as the Gaelic League, which were once a bedrock of cultural politics. It left a vacuum filled by an increasingly arrogant Catholic Church, with a post-famine project of defining and controlling the popular practices of the people at the cost of emasculating the formation of progressive movements. The vacuum at the heart of the Republic was filled by an uncritical cosmopolitanism and the mercenary acceptance of the demands of transnational capital.

In the north, some might view the problem as being the easy availability of vehicles of protest and resistance. The wave of change, which has transformed the south, has increased the ability of the fractious groups in the north to mobilise their available cultural and political capital around institutions such as the Orange Order and Sinn Féin. In the former camp, we can observe the enduring appeal of attempting to recapture the 'old' certainties that the Protestant population enjoyed during the period of direct rule. Gretta Conroy's continued embrace of her lost love Michael Furey, in 'The Dead', represents an emotionally appealing, if ultimately destructive, *riot of emotions* in contrast to the *rational, modern* and *cosmopolitan* values

---

6 www.grandorange.org.uk.

offered by her husband Gabriel. Similarly, the north's militant Protestant minority find the resonance with their romantic but 'dead' culture infinitely more powerful and alluring, compared to the cold postmodernism of the new global order they see unfettered south of the border.

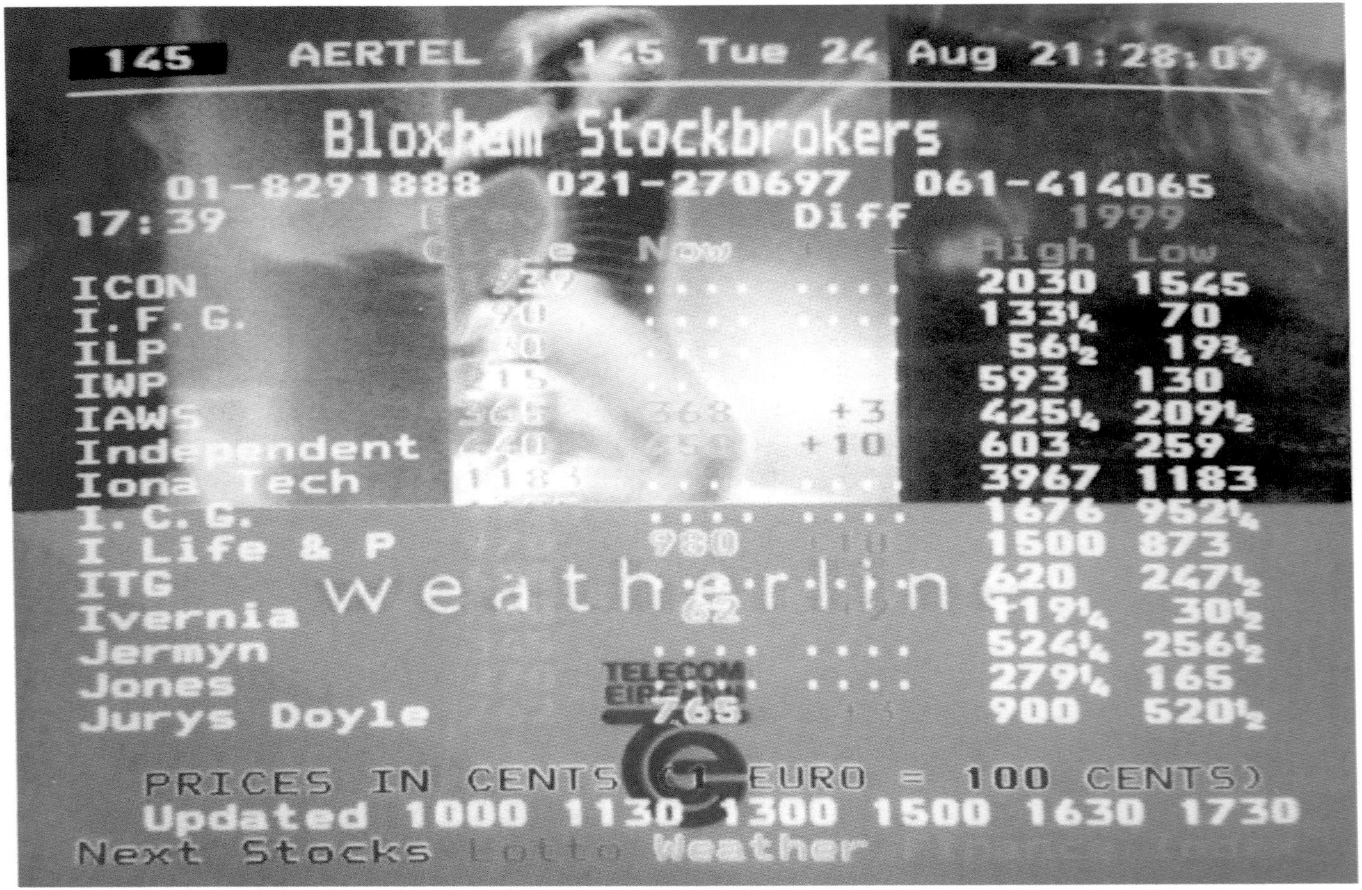
145 AERTEL 145 Tue 24 Aug 21:28:09
Bloxham Stockbrokers
01-8291888 021-270697 061-414065
17:39 Diff 1999
High Low
ICON 2030 1545
I.F.G. 133¼ 70
ILP 56½ 19¾
IWP 593 130
IAWS 368 +3 425¼ 209½
Independent +10 603 259
Iona Tech 3967 1183
I.C.G. 1676 952¼
I Life & P 980 1500 873
ITG 620 247½
Ivernia 119¼ 30½
Jermyn 524¼ 256½
Jones 279¼ 165
Jurys Doyle 765 900 520½
weatherline
TELECOM EIREANN
PRICES IN CENTS (1 EURO = 100 CENTS)
Updated 1000 1130 1300 1500 1630 1730
Next Stocks Lotto Weather

CHAPTER 18

Soft Solutions to Hard Times

SEÁN Ó RIAIN

There are many remarkable aspects of the turnaround in the Irish economy since the 1980s. The surge in foreign investment, the emergence of new information-based industries and occupations, the network of local area partnerships, the durability of national social partnership arrangements, the transformation of ways of working and of the relations between work, family and social life: these are all central elements of the so-called Celtic Tiger economy.

Perhaps the most surprising aspect, however, has been the growth of a significant sector of indigenous Irish-owned companies, often working in knowledge-intensive, high technology products and services. The Celtic Tiger appears to have brought with it a new class of technically sophisticated Irish capitalists and professionals. For the first time in its history, the Republic of Ireland can lay claim to its own national capitalist class (or they can lay claim to it). Among Irish manufacturing firms, exports increased by 19 per cent, output increased by 17 per cent and employment increased by 14 per cent between 1990 and 1996.[1] The growth of

---

1 Central Statistics Office, *Census of industrial production 1990*, Dublin: Stationery Office, 1991; Central Statistics Office, *Census of industrial production 1996*, Dublin: Stationery Office, 1997.

international services, in particular computer software, was even more impressive. The Irish-owned software sector, the topic of this chapter, is one of the leading emerging software industries in the world, alongside Israel and India. Companies such as Iona Technologies, Trintech and CBT Systems have become important international figures in their particular areas of specialisation. The software industry is also the fastest growing stripe on the Celtic Tiger's shining coat.

The comfort of understandable failures

The past might appear to be a foreign country from the perspective of Ireland in the 1990s. It is difficult to recall the desperation of the 1980s, with its mass unemployment and emigration, from the vantage point of the technical professionals and self-confident Irish capitalists of the end of the 1990s. However, it is in the 1980s that the successes of the 1990s have their roots. It is to that period we must turn to discover the origins of the transformation of the Irish economy, uncovering the initial moves towards the creation of the Irish software industry and analysing the process through which it grew and became a vital global industry in the 1990s.

This transformation is unthinkable in terms of the ways in which we had understood the Irish economy from the 1950s through the 1980s. The ultimate failure of economic development in the 1980s was explained by a vicious circle of excessive dependence on the international economy and the weakness of national institutions. Dependency theory argued that an economy focused on foreign investment could not hope to build up its national resources, as transnational corporations offered relatively few skilled jobs to their employees, provided few sales opportunities for Irish firms and repatriated their profits rather than re-investing them in Ireland.[2] Indigenous Irish firms faced the double bind of a

2 D. O'Hearn, *Inside the Celtic Tiger: The Irish economy and the Asian model*, London: Pluto Press, 1998.

domestic economy oriented towards transnational corporations and enormous barriers to entry when competing against established firms in global markets. Other commentators pointed to the weakness of public institutions in Ireland at building alternative development strategies. The Irish state bureaucracy was weak in its capacity to implement whatever policy it might formulate; while Irish politicians were embroiled in relationships of patronage and back-scratching. The failures of development based on foreign investment and the weaknesses of national institutions were linked in a vicious cycle where emigration relieved the pressure on institutions to tackle the problems of development.[3] The inability of Irish institutions to promote development was widely contrasted with the successes of the 'developmental states' of Japan, Korea and the 'Asian Tigers' in rapidly developing their economies. Failure in the pursuit of Irish economic development was both familiar to the people of Ireland and relatively well understood by its social scientists, although controversies of course remained.

However, the success of the Celtic Tiger economy threw up new challenges for commentators on the Irish economy. How could the fastest growing economy in Europe and one of the fastest growing in the world, an economy which had turned mass unemployment and emigration into rising employment and return migration, be reconciled with these understandings of the economy before the late 1980s? My research into the software industry reveals a new relationship between the state and groups within Irish society, creating an alliance that has been the basis of the indigenous software industry. A new 'virtuous circle' has emerged, re-shaping significant elements of the relationship between Irish institutions and the global economy. State agencies revealed a new flexibility, which enabled them to shape the growth of the indigenous software industry through their close ties to

---

3 L. Mjoset, *The Irish economy in a comparative institutional perspective*, Dublin: National Economic and Social Council, Report No. 93, 1992.

local technical professionals and the creation of a social world that supported industry innovation and growth. Looking at the social history of this indigenous software sector in some more detail will show the potential and limits of this state–society alliance in promoting social and economic development.

The success of the Irish software industry

The indigenous software industry began in the late 1970s with fragments – of firms, relationships and state policies – out of which a dynamic industry was forged. Economic sociology shows that economic life does not exist in isolation from social life as a whole, but that economic life and market behaviour are 'embedded' in social relationships and institutions. To create a new industry is therefore a daunting task. It is not simply a question of building up a few firms, but the challenge of creating new groups of employers, employees, public policy-makers and educators. It involves creating a new social world of relationships between employers and employees, between firms at home and abroad, among firms and state agencies.

Of course, in the late 1970s, you could have been forgiven for being pessimistic regarding the prospects for a vibrant indigenous information technology sector. Few Irish firms had gone beyond the markets that could be guaranteed for them by the state in industries such as beef and property development, while Irish professional employees had the option to pursue careers within the transnationals in Ireland or of emigrating. Moreover, the outlook of the major state agency concerned with industrial development (the Industrial Development Authority or IDA) was dominated by the needs of the transnationals. Despite their growing skill at attracting foreign investment, the subtle arts of supporting small firms drawing on indigenous resources were very much under-developed within the IDA. Why then did a durable industry develop where we would have expected collapse in the face of free trade, foreign investment and emigration?

The earliest traces of the social context of Irish software are to be found in the mid-to-late 1970s. A small number of firms emerged, based around early state investments in attracting transnationals and upgrading telecommunications and education. Clusters of specialisation developed around finance and banking (primarily based on sales to transnationals), telecommunications (stimulated in part by the upgrading of telecoms in the early 1980s) and computer-based training and systems software (prompted in different ways by the expansion of technical education). These small groups of software developers and entrepreneurs were in a very vulnerable state in these early years, living from contract to contract in the midst of a recession which was decimating the country as a whole. Nevertheless, it was out of these humble beginnings that Irish software was born.

The IDA focus, from the late 1970s, on attracting software transnationals had an impact, although few came before 1985 when Microsoft and Lotus arrived. The major contribution of the IDA policy was the investment in electrical engineering and computer science third-level education. However, the mass emigration continued in the 1980s with 40 to 50 per cent of engineering students and 20 to 30 per cent of computer science graduates leaving within a year of getting their degree. Although the goal of this policy was to entice foreign investment, a number of these students did make their way into the Irish-owned software firms, joining forces with a small core of industry veterans. State policy to attract transnationals had the largely unintended consequence therefore of helping to create the technical professional labour force that would form the basis of indigenous software.

This tightknit and little-known social world within Irish society became one of its most celebrated elements by the 1990s. State actions, which developed the industry's capabilities without smothering its social ground, were critical. An alliance developed between the newly emerging firms and key people in a range of more marginal state agencies: the National Board for Science and Technology, Eolas, the National Software Centre and later Forbairt and the National

Software Directorate. Close ties developed between these key individuals and industry. Indeed, some of their careers overlapped between the public and private sectors; such individuals include all the directors of the National Software Centre and the National Software Directorate, the primary agencies with responsibility for the software industry since the mid-1980s. These state agencies came to support the emerging firms, while the growth of the indigenous industry over time came to legitimise the state agencies. The IDA had come in for heavy criticism during the crisis of the 1980s and was no longer able to dominate completely the industrial policy agenda. The problems of the 1980s, therefore, ironically created some political and organisational space for strategies other than attracting foreign investment.

Concretely, state agencies contributed in a number of ways. Firstly, they helped to define the industry as one focused on software products for export, which had much greater potential for long-term innovation than programming services. They achieved this by targeting grant-aid on firms carrying out this type of work. Secondly, they used the grant-aid mechanism and the relationships developed with firms to build up firms' capabilities – to 'make winners'. The state agencies provided small companies with critical financial support when the banks and other private-sector financiers were unwilling to take the risk. Grants were tied in part to research and development, management training, marketing and so on, while the state agencies also encouraged firms to network with one another and with industry 'mentors' who could guide them through the challenges of growth and international competition. Thirdly, state agencies were instrumental in the creation of a network of centres of innovation, programmes in advanced technologies, industry associations and so on. These institutions were typically located in the universities and governed by an alliance of business, state agencies and educators. The state agencies were therefore simultaneously engaged in creating new social actors, the firms of the software industry, and in supporting the relationships between these actors. They did that by building up a web of associations and social ties that supported information-sharing and co-operation.

This social infrastructure has been critical to Irish software firms, as many are very small and rely heavily on contacts and relationships within the industry for crucial information, resources and business. They are very densely networked with one another and with international firms. This has resulted in a situation where the industry has flourished despite the lack of any very large or particularly dominant firms. The industry in fact consists of a large network of smaller firms (less than 20 employees) and a number of star performers such as Iona Technologies and Trintech which have developed significant strengths in international markets.

The supports provided by state agencies for development and industry networking have been critical to both sides of the industry. These supports have been effective because they are based on a close but dynamic relationship between the industry and the state agencies. The state agencies are able to push the firms to improve themselves due to what Peter Evans has called 'embedded autonomy': the state officials are 'embedded' in industry through their close social ties but remain 'autonomous' from industry due to the demands of objectivity and performance within the state bureaucracy and the constant reshuffling of state agencies which has broken some of the over-cosy relationships that have existed.[4] Successful economic development has therefore depended on effective support from social and political institutions, and this in turn has only been possible because of the particular form of the relationship between state and industry. It turns out that we cannot understand the success of Irish industry and the Celtic Tiger economy without paying attention to the many ways in which economic life is 'embedded' in social and political relations and institutions.

---

4 P. Evans, *Embedded autonomy*, Princeton: Princeton University Press, 1995.

Globalisation, inequality and grown-up tigers

The great success story of the Irish economy since the mid-1980s has been based therefore on the social embeddedness of economic action, not on the operation of theoretically free markets. The indigenous software industry developed in an extremely open economy, facing the opportunities and constraints of trade, foreign investment and migration. However, this exposure to the global economy did not in and of itself determine the fate of the Irish industry. Globalisation does not necessarily spell doom, as dependency theory suggests, nor success, as orthodox economics suggests. A great deal depends on how social institutions link a nation's firms and workers to the global economy in very specific ways. In the Irish case, the state has played a crucial role in the development process. But Ireland is no Japan, Korea or even Singapore where the 'developmental state' takes a more direct guiding role. Instead, the Irish state relies on managing the connections between local firms and the global economy, on building sustainable social relationships within the industry and on being responsive to changing economic conditions through a flexible organisational structure.

Ireland then is a 'flexible developmental state'. This flexible model of state-shaping of the economy has its benefits and its drawbacks. On the one hand, such a state is well positioned to adjust to changes in local society and the global economy and to promote development by effectively integrating local firms and workers into international markets and workplaces. On the other hand, the state relinquishes any role in shaping the global economy itself, taking as a given the increasing power of corporations and income inequality internationally. This is exacerbated by the unequal development of state–society alliances within Ireland itself. We have seen how state agencies, now gathered together under Enterprise Ireland, worked closely to support the development of local technical entrepreneurs and professionals, creating a global professional class within Ireland. Unionised workers fared less well, sacrificing a great deal in terms of pay in order to restore macroeconomic health, only to find in the late 1990s that the success of the global professional class was increasing wage inequality rapidly[5] and making owning a home an impossibility for many of their children. Finally, those at the lower ends of the socio-economic distribution fared badly. They have fallen behind the rest of the country in terms of income and standards of living, as welfare payments and household consumption rose sluggishly and poverty rates decreased only slightly.

A sociological perspective can provide valuable insights, therefore, into the real story behind the success of Irish industry over the past ten years or so. It can help us to understand better the Irish model of development, in order to sustain and build upon it. However, it can also give us an insight into the limits of the Irish development model. We have seen that even the most resourceful of social groups can benefit hugely from state support. The Irish state must focus domestically on applying its efforts at developing the capabilities of society more equally. Furthermore, the state should look to its role in international bodies such as the EU in terms of supporting a regulated process of economic globalisation, with limits on the power of capital and an effective social floor set to competition. A political project, whether it be at the national or global level, which relies on separating economic life from social life will prove not only unequal and unjust but also inefficient.

---

5 A. Barrett, T. Callan and B. Nolan, 'Rising wage inequality. Returns to education and labour market institutions: evidence from Ireland', *British Journal of Industrial Relations*, vol. 37, no. 1, 1999, pp. 77–100.

CHAPTER 19

When the *Local* goes Global

EAMONN SLATER

On 10 October 1998, it was announced that the first Irish pub in Buenos Aires had opened. According to the report, Guinness had opened 1,700 Irish pubs since 1992.[1] The Irish pub has truly gone global. There are Irish pubs in as diverse locations as Abu Dhabi, Reykjavik, Shanghai and in other metropolitan centres located in forty-two countries around the world. This reflects a growing global trend in the popularity of all things Irish. Irish actors, authors, musicians and poets have become household names all over the world. The Irish pub seems to be following in their footsteps. However, unlike people, the pub is a stationary object occupying a definite space and cannot easily 'export' itself. Therefore, if the Irish pub is to travel it can only do so as a simulated entity. But this entity can move and does move.

According to Lash and Urry, one of the features of late modernity is that more objects flow through global space. These flows consist of capital, labour, commodities, information and images. The Irish pub demonstrates flows of commodity and images, but with one crucial difference, that it is a re-created space for the consumption of goods, which are both local and global. And like these other global

---

1 'Irish pub in Argentina', *The Irish Times*, 10 October 1998.

objects, their image (design process) is crucial to their success.[2] This chapter is an attempt to understand how this construct has been exported as a physical and a cultural object. This will, I hope, help us to throw light not only on how we are constructing our Irish identity but also on how we are 'globalising' our 'local'.

The hybridisation of 'Muddy Murphys'

In 1998 there were three Irish pubs in Singapore, the most recent of which was Muddy Murphys. It occupies a two-storey premises in the Orchard Hotel shopping complex, which is located in the middle of Singapore's busy enter-tainment area. Upstairs looks like an old traditional pub combined with a grocery, while the downstairs has the appearance of an eighteenth-century cottage. Its name, Muddy Murphys, reflects the necessary hybridisation of Irish culture with the native culture. Muddy is easily pronounced in the vernacular, while Murphy is Ireland's most common name. The cultural differences and their subsequent hybrid-isation are also expressed on a spatial dimension. Upstairs, with its high ceiling and a greater sense of space, the clientele is 80 per cent local; while in the 'cosy' country cottage downstairs, the crowd is generally composed of British and Irish ex-pats.[3] Therefore, the success of this pub is being determined by an attempt to get the right balance between tuning in to local market needs and retaining the essentially Irish atmosphere. In this necessary mix, there is no possibility of creating an authentic Irish pub.

If the issue of authenticity arises, it is merely concerned with how the customers accept (or reject) the concept of Irishness presented to them. And this sense of Irishness is not exclusively maintained by the decor alone but is also

---

2 S. Lash and J. Urry, *Economies of signs and space*, London: Sage Publications, 1994, p. 15.
3 S. Linder, 'Muddy Murphys cleans up', *The Buzz*, issue 2, 1998, pp. 26–27.

'staged' through other levels of performance. For example, with regard to customer service there is an attempt to instil an Irish approach, but there is a problem with so few Irish-born staff. The solution to this problem is again sought in ensuring a 'balance of authenticity':

> Our staff are informal and relaxed, they engage well with everyone, and, even though it's a way of dealing with people that isn't usual in Asia, the locals love it.[4]

Most of the staff are Singaporean with only one Irish ex-pat, the manager. However, the owner is keen to add another ex-pat to ensure the 'balance of authenticity'.

Food production is also delicately balanced. Food is supplied by four local Chinese chefs, who have created their own Muddy Murphys' speciality: chilli crab with potato wedges. Although there is little sense of it in this speciality, Irishness is not completely excluded from the menu in this pub. Irish stew is served during the day and every St Patrick's Day the pub holds its own oyster-opening festival. The Irishness of the event is maintained not just by holding it on this particular day of days but also in awarding the prize. The winner goes to Ireland to compete at the Galway Oyster Festival.

Finally, Irish music bands, mainly traditional, are mixed with Australian bands, which provide a 'more contemporary sound'. Recorded music is also played – 60 per cent pop and 40 per cent traditional Irish. Therefore, hybridisation is the crucial element in achieving this 'balance of authenticity'.

This process of hybridisation implies that the sense of Irishness needs to penetrate as many activities and objects as possible in order to create and re-create an Irish identity. As a consequence, an object, which would normally perform a single function in an ordinary pub, now may take on a secondary role in a themed pub. In the case of Muddy Murphys, objects have to become totems of Irish identity. To

---

4 S. Linder, ibid., p. 27.

act as a totem, Irishness, either as a word, image or symbol, must be actually inscribed on all available surfaces. This is why images, symbols and words associated with Ireland seem to appear ad nauseum. A sense of the absurd can arise. For example, on the wall in Muddy Murphys the price list reads as follows:

MUDDY MURPHYS
Biachlár
'Best prices lads!'

Pint Guinness $12
¹/₂ Guinness $8

A number of Irish connotations may be read in this notice. Besides the brand names – Muddy Murphys and Guinness – there is the use of the Gaelic word, biachlár. However, it is misused in this context as it translates as the 'food menu' rather than a drinks price list. Secondly, the use of the word 'lads' in the hand-written phrase 'Best prices lads!', is a typical Irish colloquialism used by people who are on extremely good terms with each other. In this case, its use suggests a familiarity between the staff and a core group of customers. This confirms in a visual way, the informal style of service associated with being Irish. The over-penetration of 'all things Irish' and their subsequent structure as a narrative within such a limited space creates a sense of hyper-reality. The mixing of Gaelic, English, Hiberno-English and American (dollar signs) reiterates this characteristic of informality and contributes to the construction of the sense of Irishness. The sense of informality is also evident in the physical layout of the design.

The logic behind bric-a-brac and nooks and crannies

According to Karen O'Sullivan, an expert on the interior design of Irish pubs:

The design creates the atmosphere and the atmosphere creates the mood and ambience that entices the customer to relax and, most importantly, to return.[5]

Designing the Irish pub seems to involve a necessary illusion: it should appear as though no design has gone into it at all. Haphazardness is the order of the day, achieved by the display of bric-a-brac, which is apparently hidden away in nooks and crannies throughout the pub. In the Irish pub *Fado* in Chicago, one writer discovered a loom hanging from a ceiling, elsewhere he found a spinning wheel, a butter churn, a wash stand, farm tools, seed bags and a collection of buckets and bottles. The bric-a-brac even includes branded commodities in this re-creation of a post office/grocery/bar:

> A telephone switchboard is set in the corner, and stacked on the shelves are boxes of Jacobs cream crackers and Oxo cubes, bags of Mosse's brown bread mix, and jars of Fruitfield marmalade. Adverts for Players cigarettes, Marsh Co's biscuits and Wills's Cut Gold Bar tobacco hung from the walls.[6]

The display of these commodities on the shelves acts not only as a visual curiosity to all but can also trigger personal memories for those who were exposed to these images and commodities in the past. For the latter, these objects become encapsulated in memories of a personal past and may in fact create a sense of longing for that past. In general the bric-a-brac successfully assists the customer to identify with the surroundings in a positive way. Accordingly, the brand names of goods on display are not about advertising or 'branding' the Irish identity – they are about creating a sense of nostalgia. A longing is created for an idealised place and time beyond the immediate concerns of modernity. The design

5 S. Linder, 'Design', *The Buzz*, issue 4, 1999, p. 25.
6 J. Arndorfer, 'Ireland, the theme park', *The Editor*, 18 June 1999, p. 13.

and image on the packaging of these goods look quaint and simple in comparison to the sophistication and slick display of contemporary commodities. In a sense, they, as 'aestheticised' objects, still maintain a sense of desirability, not now for consumption but for a flight of fantasy. The logic of the theme park is revealed in the illogical arrangement of these displays. In the following photograph we have an example of objects being displayed out of context.

Irish memorabilia, Copenhagen[7]

Here, hanging from the ceiling is an Irish flag and a road sign. What is interesting about these types of memorabilia is that in normal circumstances they would appear outside a pub rather than inside. Their change of physical location indicates that they are now performing a different role. They

7 The author would like to thank Bill Nelson for this photograph.

provide the necessary material conditions for the construction of a narrative around the theme of Irishness. They focus attention onto this particular theme and in doing so they 'frame' the experience people get from the pub. But pub themes can be mixed, as in the new pub, The Kilkenny, in Buenos Aires:

> The Retiro district is named after its famous railway station, imported from Britain 150 years ago, and it was decided that The Kilkenny should keep to the railway theme, taking the Irish Victorian design and using it to re-create an Irish Victorian railway station. The theme is embellished with a number of original items shipped from Ireland: old train timetables, station clocks and signs. More importantly, the pub features an original station waiting room, while food is served in an original first class dining coach.[8]

Hybridisation of cultures at its finest! What is interesting in the above quotation is how original Irish items were collected and shipped to Argentina. But this collection of Irish bric-a-brac is not haphazard. Its casual deployment in the nooks and crannies of these Irish pubs belies the fact that the entire performance is orchestrated by big business.

Behind the irrational appearance lies the rationale of big business

There are four companies in Ireland who are approved by Guinness to design and build 'authentic' Irish pubs around the world. Another company, Interiors Trading Company, set up in 1998, collects and sells bric-a-brac worldwide. In their £3 million showroom, they have original and reproduction antiques, but also salvaged items like glass screens, printing presses, fireplaces and various types of flooring.

---

8   S. Linder, 'Latin America opens up!', *The Buzz*, issue 4, 1999, p. 23.

They scour Ireland and the world for items of Irish interest and other exotic objects. For they too have become global and now offer to supply exotic items to any themed enterprise worldwide. You do not have to come to their warehouse in Finglas, Dublin, to view these bric-a-brac objects as they are listed and photographed in a catalogue on the company's website.

The four companies can now design, manufacture, ship and install a unit in nearly any part of the globe within, on average, three months. The major company in this field is the Irish Pub Company, who boast that they are responsible for the appearance of 1,600 of these global Irish pubs. They have five basic categories of design. The cottage pub is meant to reflect the 'Irish idea that a pub is an extension of the living room'. It has a strong sense of intimacy, which is encouraged by low ceilings and a maze of nooks and crannies. The old tradition of serving drinks in shops, chemists and even undertakers is the basis of the shop-front style. From the Victorian period, comes the Victorian pub with its high ceilings and mahogany furnishings. The Gaelic pub is meant to evoke Irish history. And finally, there is the Brewery pub based on St James' Gate brewery in Dublin, the original home of Guinness. These five basic designs form a template for the Irish pub concept. These designs may be combined within the one premises, as is the case in Muddy Murphys in Singapore, where the old cottage layout on the ground floor is complemented with a Victorian pub upstairs.

Nothing is left to chance. Even the Irish warm welcome is being constructed on a scientific basis. Because of the necessity of providing an Irish style of service, recruitment of Irish staff has become a vital component in the Irish pub concept. To help overcome this global difficulty, a recruitment firm, Contract Catering Personnel, was established in Galway in 1997. This company utilises a network of trade contacts throughout Ireland. In selecting candidates, the agency puts special emphasis on 'meeting and greeting' personality profiles and presentation, and makes special use of psychometric testing. This is a complex process of evaluating relevant personality traits – such as people orientation, versatility, resilience and communication skills – on a scientific basis.[9] But all of this effort has been worthwhile for at least some. According to a representative of the Irish Pub Company, they have created fifty to sixty millionaires around the world as a result of 'theming' their pub into an Irish pub.

But the process of theming does not begin nor end at our shores, as it is also taking place in our own pub culture.

'Brand' pubs within

Theme pubs are also appearing in Ireland, but not as exclusively Irish theme pubs. There are a great variety of them in Dublin. Pravda on Liffey Street depicts the Russian Revolution with huge wall murals. Zanzibar on Ormond Quay is like a cross between a Middle Eastern souk and a colonial gentlemen's club in Tangiers. The revamped Pembroke Bar now harks back to 1930s Barcelona for inspiration. According to John Young, the reason for the emergence of these new pubs on the streets of Dublin is twofold:

> Many of this new breed of publican emerged six or seven years ago with the instigation of Designated Areas Incentive by the government. This resulted in property developers entering the market initially as developers of property which in turn gave them an entrée into the liquor trade which was tax efficient. Also, as a result of these people travelling abroad they brought back to Ireland concepts by way of avant-garde architectural and design creation that resulted in the so-called yuppie bars.[10]

The aim of these new theme pubs is to appeal to particular groups of customers. For example, there are bars for the

---

9 'The World's best bar staff on tap', *The Buzz*, issue 1, 1998.
10 John Young is quoted in J. Daly, 'The Irish Publican Army', *Irish Independent, Weekend Supplement*, 5 June 1999, p. 22.

young professionals, family bars, student bars, gay bars and sports bars. The market in Ireland and beyond is being segmented in ways similar to other consumer sectors, such as tourism and magazine publishing. And this process of market segmentation is being created through the construction of particular images and themes.

Irishness is just one theme among many circulating as object in the global market. In consequence, the 'theming' of Irish pubs in Ireland and abroad is all about finding niche markets for new commodities on a global scale. Tapping into the niche market is now being attempted on the level of the visual. Creating atmosphere is not just about attracting the right customers to one's premises and in doing so creating an identity for the pub, it is now about physically changing the built environment in order to embed that identity in physical structures. It is this latter trend that has allowed the Irish 'local' to go global and in doing so we have exported another cultural object to be consumed by the global market.

CHAPTER 20

Virtual Locality

RUTH CASEY

Although not its real name, Ballygannive is a village on the western seaboard of Ireland. We will get a sense of what the place and its people are like. It constitutes a strange place, for it is deeply shaped by global processes. The peculiarity of Ballygannive as a locality is that a high proportion of the people who stay there have come from outside. What is local and what is global interpenetrate in ways that have produced Ballygannive.

Roland Robertson contends that, far from being opposed to each other, local and global are closely linked: what is called local is to a large degree constructed on a global basis. It is not that global processes simply supersede or eradicate local features in a drive for uniformity. 'From my own analytical and interpretative standpoint the concept of globalisation has involved the simultaneity and the interpenetration of what are conventionally called the global and the local . . .'.[1] Globalisation involves the 'invention' of localities; it also opens up the possibility of mobilising and manipulating global processes for local purposes.

---

1 R. Robertson, 'Globalisation: Time-space and homogeneity and heterogeneity', in M. Featherstone, S. Lash and R. Robertson (eds.), *Global modernities*, London: Sage, 1995, p. 30.

A *community of flows*

Ballygannive has witnessed the progressive decline of the local population. But it continues to attract an 'outsider' population. These outsiders are divided into blow-ins, visitors and tourists, according to the level of contact with the locality. Tourists form a passing trade, a group which is 'ripped-off' by the local population. Visitors comprise a returning category that are welcomed and recognised. Blow-ins enjoy as much respect as locals do. The locals view outsiders as active agents impacting upon the community in economic and cultural terms.

Some residents own a holiday home in the locality. Shaw and Williams make a distinction between second homes and weekend homes.[2] Weekend homes provide a haven from the weekly work routine associated with the smaller apartment, while second homes are located in a more distant region. Shaw and Williams conclude that the former tend to have a greater economic and cultural impact than the latter. This is explained in terms of the additional custom to local services and greater involvement in community life characteristic of weekend homes. Those staying in holiday homes do not mingle with the community, save to buy the odd necessity. The vast majority of holiday homes in Ballygannive are second homes. Of the new houses currently being built in Ballygannive, around two-thirds will be for people from elsewhere in Ireland and abroad, while one-third will be for returning locals. Ballygannive has benefited in a very positive way from its holiday homes and they are welcomed by the local community. In a local resident's opinion, 'they obviously lend a bit of atmosphere' to the village.

In the caravan sites (one of which is situated on the dunes, while the other is towards the furthest end of the village) reside the tourists who spend up to two months in the area. The main focus for both young and old is the beach, which provides a safe haven for children. During this time, the

---

2 G. Shaw and A. M. Williams, *Critical issues in tourism*, Oxford: Blackwell, 1994, pp. 235–6.

pub is kept busy throughout the day and far into the night. Links between these outsiders and locals are created and strengthened with the swapping of news and stories from new and old friends. The presence of a band in the lounge area of the pub on weekends provides a festive atmosphere. But its isolation from the major towns ten miles either way makes Ballygannive a family-oriented holiday, rather than a resort holiday. The locals are keen to maintain this image, through admission of children to the pub even on crowded nights, upkeep of the beach and pony rides for children. Local perception of Ballygannive as an isolated village serves to distance it from more commercialised areas.

B&Bs cater for the passing tourist, with the average stay limited to one or two nights duration. Unlike the family-oriented holiday associated with the caravan sites, the B&Bs attract a much broader spectrum of tourists, ranging from walkers to insect and butterfly specialists. This type of tourist tends to be actively interested in the physical environment, engaging in rock climbing, pony trekking, caving and cycling. Generally, they have little or no contact with the local community, maximising the amount of activities possible into one day while passing through. Directions are requested to nearby attractions, or information demanded of the area. The B&Bs and restaurant open their doors from Easter until 1st October, although the tourist season proper lasts from July through to the end of August. Each of the B&Bs are signposted along the main route, but are not affiliated with Bord Fáilte. One B&B is advertised in two American travel guides only, not in Ireland. Heavy reliance, therefore, is placed on attracting those tourists travelling through the village to stay.

A fourth category includes the coach tourists, who come in search of a learning holiday. Travelling from Germany and Holland, they are interested in the botanical features of Ballygannive. Most have a background in gardening and come to Ireland to examine its gardens. The day coach, which takes the botany enthusiasts around the area, stops in Ballygannive to delight in Nature's own garden. Two locals operate as tour guides for the coaches, educating and showing the tourists particular sites in Ballygannive.

Summer, for the permanent residents of Ballygannive, is a busy season. It hails the return of the local youth from England and America with the prospect of helping out on family farms or finding employment in the various B&Bs. The pub is filled with the chat of old friends lingering over a pint until well into the night. While the older locals welcome the chance to reminisce over past times, the younger crowd gathers around returning friends. Against this background is the incessant shriek of playful children, who dart around the lounge area under the watchful eye of their parents.

The influx of coach tours, cars and vans, extending to horse rides through the roads and down onto the beach, heralds an approaching tourist season. The local services – such as B&Bs with en-suite bathrooms, the riding centre, shop/post-office, pub, two caravan sites, restaurant and church – are all positioned along the one road. They define Ballygannive as a stopping point in the tourist flow to the major destination towns. Each of the services boasts parking facilities just off the road, which visually attract the tourist from the road, either to check a map or to gaze upon the landscape from the car while passing through the village, or lure the tourist into the respective services. Plans for petrol pumps and a café, to be located at a strategic point, are intended to attract and detain the tourist passing through the village. Ballygannive has come to define itself in terms of its tourist flows.

Local revival

Local attitudes towards the place have been influenced by its global perception as a fairytale location in the west of Ireland by the sea:

> I think the best compliment of all . . . that could be paid to Ballygannive, is the number of people who want to come and live here . . . from the outside, y'know.

Still, I think tourism [is] very important – and it is important for them [the locals], I think, to see people coming, passing through. Because I think that in itself is a kind of a lift to them y'know. I think it helps them to appreciate what they have.

The local priest has noted the increase in the amount of weddings taking place in Ballygannive. The number of locals getting married has decreased, so the increase is entirely due to outsiders. Visitors, who have come to Ballygannive or around previously on holiday, return in order to get married in the parish. He recalls one French couple in particular who asked him to marry them in a local church. On the day of the wedding, he and the organist turned up to an empty church. Half an hour later the bride and groom arrived, distraught, as they had thought that another church they had seen in the area was the parish church.

Local perception of the value of Ballygannive is also heightened by outsider interest in the land. While the disinterest expressed by the local youths about the duties and obligations associated with the agricultural land persists, outsider interest in the land serves to validate and vindicate a time-honoured tradition in the eyes of the older locals. In recent years, some of the youths have returned to Ballygannive from the urban centres, having realised its worth as a place and a community.

The locality is given its value mainly through the positive assessment that visitors make of it. In fact, the very fabric of the locality relies more and more on outsiders. Set dancing has experienced a huge revival and it is practised with fervour in the local pub, where classes are offered to all. A non-local from Holland has been teaching the Irish dance to the locals for the past two winters with such success that classes were offered to the children at the national school last winter. The Wildlife Convention and the Fishing Competition were dying events; the locals had lost the incentive and the energy to push their potential. They were reactivated by newcomers to Ballygannive – returning locals from travels abroad, coming home to settle with their new families, or people coming to start afresh in Ballygannive, having lived abroad. Crucially now, they are pushing for and organising these events:

> Ballygannive is really . . . since I spoke to you last there's so much happening here. There are three and four evenings a week where they're at something, which is a whole new thing. I mean, there was nothing for them years ago. Not a thing. And now there's . . . we're really busy and it's great!

Significantly then, it is the influence of the outsiders that is creating the community feel. They uphold the uniqueness of Ballygannive; they vindicate the lifestyle pattern and choices of the locals. 'They [tourists] say it's beautiful and you somehow feel responsible for how beautiful it is.' Through them, locals have come to value Ballygannive and their own lifestyle.

Global networking

During the summer, events are organised to attract tourists rather than just entertain the locals. The Wildlife Convention provides such an example, as its lecture-style format offers a specialised insight into aspects of the wildlife of the locality. The convention is held for one week in May and in September, thus lengthening the tourist season at both ends of the summer. Although the local community is freely invited, few if any turn up, with the result that the convention is heavily dominated by American, German, Dutch and French visitors. The Fishing Competition constituted a major attraction in former years. The shore-angling festivities beckoned fishermen nationwide and abroad for two weeks in June and July.

In mid-July of every year, the Charismatic Week is held in Ballygannive. Up to 500 people come from the north, south, east and west of Ireland, to stay in one of the caravan sites. During the week, the charismatics are encouraged to sleep under canvas in true pilgrim fashion. As this frequently entails sleeping under howling winds and lashing rain, this motto bears true meaning! Those ranging in age between mid-teens and late twenties come in large groups and stay in large army tents, while the older charismatics reside in the comfort of the caravans. As families and parental figures occupy the caravans, for the most part there is little interaction between those in tents and those in caravans. The meeting ground for all charismatics is the church, to progress later on to the pub where both locals and charismatics mingle. Each night a procession of the rosary leads the way barefoot from the dunes to the church for a two-and-a-half-hour Mass. At one stage during the week, an outdoor Mass is celebrated either on the riverbank or on a large slab of limestone rock overlooking the ocean. As the pamphlet emphasises 'Walking with the Lord', the charismatics are actively encouraged to walk the paths, seek peace and serenity at the water's edge, or climb the mountain.

The local youths are constantly around the caravan site, mingling with the younger charismatics. During Masses, the priest encourages both locals and visitors to collectively gaze upon the landscape in evocation of divine inspiration. Through their involvement in a ritual of gaze and prayer the locals are accepting and endorsing the outsider definition of Ballygannive as a place of spirituality.

Each of these events, the Wildlife Convention, Fishing Competition and Charismatic Week, are networked outside of Ballygannive. In its prime, the Fishing Competition was advertised through a newsletter to friends both in Ireland and abroad. In later years, the Wildlife Convention has attracted much interest. A local man organises lecturers and guests, sending newsletters and brochures to friends in America and in Ireland. His winter months are spent abroad in America, travelling between states, visiting friends who, in turn, usually spend some part of the summer in Ballygannive. By dint of a personal letter, circulated on a quarterly basis by the local priest, the charismatics are kept abreast of any reunions or masses held during the year. Tapes of the recorded music are sold, capturing the songs at each mass as a steadfast memory of the Charismatic Week. Through a network of letters, brochures and even tapes, contact is maintained between visitors and locals.

The various descriptions of Ballygannive, of its physical attributes and its atmosphere, have been internalised by the locals. This heightened awareness of Ballygannive leads to the development of an environment culture, a crucial aspect of eco-tourism, whereby the environment first becomes a value and then a commodity. Recognition of this environment culture by the locals is vital; it determines how the locals use the environment within the various businesses: the riding centre, the caravan sites, the nature reserve. In short, the locals are using their ecological resources as potential market commodities. However, this process of commodification presupposes a foreknowledge of the market, one which is gained through experience outside of Ballygannive. This knowledge is more likely to be possessed by those locals who have returned from travels or outsiders with an experience in markets abroad who have come to Ballygannive to start up a business. They have come to Ballygannive with the knowledge and awareness of how and what to develop commercially. This implies that those without this insight into the market will be unable to realise the potential of the environment at their disposal. Moreover, they will show no interest in the resources themselves.

Only the outsider's gaze is able to perceive the locality as what it may become: a landscape with an appeal to people with specialised tastes and interests. It must as such be signposted to specific niche markets abroad. A crucial aspect of this process is the ability to network through global contacts. The use of computers and electronic communication ensures continuing access to these niche markets.

A couple arrived in Ballygannive with the innovative idea to create their own software package, designing web pages. As their work base is now located in the village, they have become the informed word on computers within the village. The presence of this global industry in the locality has created interest among locals to such an extent that some of them attend computer classes held in the nearest town. The classes were fully booked due to the increased demand in the area. Most houses in Ballygannive would have a computer, as do all the tourist-related businesses in the area. One can clearly identify eagerness on the part of the locals to tie themselves into the global context through the use of computers. The success of the various businesses in Ballygannive has rested on their ability to access niche markets through global networking.

The reliance on global links does not operate in one direction only, with the locals creating and mobilising global networks. It can also work the other way round. For instance, visitors extend an invitation to their home:

> The people that have Bed and Breakfast houses, it's quite noticeable. They've smartened up an awful lot because of their dealings with tourism. It has made a whole lot of difference to them and very often, good quality guests would even invite the people from the Bed and Breakfast houses to their homes for a holiday or a break.

People who had visited the riding centre would write or send back photographs of themselves, often with one of the staff, taken on the beach in Ballygannive. A high number of people come to the centre from abroad on the recommendation of friends. This landscape is framed in a context of familiarity between tourist and local, and this becomes a major part in the memory of the tourist's visit to Ireland.

Conclusion

Rather than just a place, Ballygannive represents a stage in a flow or even, more simply, a moment in time. The passing cars provide the metaphor for this locality. It has become a configuration of people who, from the wider world, are passing through. The place has become a virtual locality, for very little is left when these global flows are abstracted. It acquires its substance, its materiality, through its link with global processes; it is revived and sustained by them. Despite the fact that it now exists mainly through its links with global processes, the challenge of this locality, and perhaps its very survival, hangs on its ability to detain the flows, even for a fleeting moment. To allow time to admire the scenery from a roadside café or time to settle for a while.